The Lost Meaning of
Classical Architecture

The Lost Meaning of Classical Architecture

Speculations
on Ornament from
Vitruvius to Venturi

George Hersey

The MIT Press
Cambridge, Massachusetts
London, England

This book was set in Baskerville
by Graphic Composition
and printed and bound
in the United States of America.

Library of Congress Cataloging-in-Publication Data

Hersey, George L.
The lost meaning of classical architecture:
speculations on ornament from
Vitruvius to Venturi / George Hersey.
p. cm.
Bibliography: p.
Includes index.
ISBN 0-262-08170-9.
ISBN 0-262-58089-6 (pbk.)
1. Decoration and ornament, Architectural.
2. Architecture, Classical.
3. Classicism in architecture.
4. Vitruvius Pollio. De architectura.
5. Architecture, Classical—Terminology.
I. Title.
NA3340.H47 1988
729′.326dc19
87-21318 CIP

10 9 8 7

To Ibycus

In general we no longer understand architecture. . . .[An] atmosphere of inexhaustible meaningfulness hung about [an ancient] building like a magic veil. Beauty entered the system only secondarily, without impairing the basic feeling of uncanny sublimity, of sanctification by magic or the gods' nearness. At most the beauty tempered the *dread*—but this dread was the prerequisite everywhere.

Friedrich Nietzsche, *Human, All-too-Human*

Contents

Acknowledgments

This book began as a series of presentations, made years ago, in Vincent Scully's Yale graduate seminar in architectural theory. I am grateful to the instructor and students in that course for their suggestions and criticisms. I am particularly grateful to Vincent Scully (again) for his classic *The Earth, the Temple and the Gods*, which started me on the road that led to this book. I would also like to thank Creighton Gilbert, Joseph Rykwert, Walter Cahn, Victor Bers, Lawrence Lowic, Alan Plattus, Jeffrey Hurwit, and J. J. Pollitt for carefully reading earlier versions of the manuscript (in part or as a whole) and for their comments. Other readers and critics, who remain nameless to me because of the publishers' delicacy, have also been helpful. Any remaining shortcomings in the book are solely my fault. I also thank Vasily Rudich, Susan Ryan, Silvia Meloni, Dietrich von Bothmer, and (for bringing the book's epigraph to my attention) Rob Anderson. Small parts of it have been read at conferences, or have appeared in publications, as will be noted in the appropriate places. I have used the Vitruvius text established by V. Rose (Leipzig: Teubner, 1899). I have also employed the translation made for the Loeb Library by Frank Granger (Cambridge, Massachusetts, 1955), but with many emendations.

1

Troping Ornament

For many years I have been asking myself the following question: Why do we still use the classical orders? Practically every town of decent size in the Western world has its quota of Doric, Ionic, and Corinthian. And some of the greatest modern buildings, from the Panthéon in Paris, to the Capitol in Washington, to the Imperial Palace in Tokyo, across Southeast Asian countries that have practically nothing to do with classical civilization, and back around the world to the government structures of Leningrad, Warsaw, and Brussels, are monumental essays in the use of the orders. Greco-Roman classicism was not only the architecture of the Greeks and Romans and of their empires, it was also the architecture, mutatis mutandis, of Romanesque Europe and of Byzantium, of the Renaissance and the Baroque, of Neoclassicism, the Baroque Revival, the Beaux-Arts, and fascism; and it is even, in a peculiar but strong way, a contributor to postmodernism.

Why? Why do architects erect columns and temple fronts derived ultimately from ancient Greek temples, when ancient Greek religion has been dead for centuries, when the temples themselves were not even buildings in the sense that they housed human activities, and when the way of life they expressed is extinct?

It all becomes even more curious when we reflect on the actual content of this architecture and meditate on the names of its ornamental components. Why at great expense do we have stone-carvers make replicas of beads, reels, eggs, darts, claws, and a type of prickly plant, the acanthus, that grows only in certain parts of the Peloponnese? Why wrap a courthouse in what an ancient Greek would interpret as the garlands or streamers used to decorate sacrificial oxen? Why call a gable by the name of a bone and leather drum, tympanum, that was used in Bacchic rituals? Why construct a crest for this drum and call it an eagle, ἀετός? Why set this drum and its eagle on humanoid supports decked in the trappings of animal sacrifice (that is to say, columns)? As Pugin, the great anti-classicist, asked, "Do we worship the blood of bulls and goats?"[1]

I cannot produce full answers to these questions, but can perhaps come closer than others have done before. I do so by examining Greek and Greco-Roman architectural terminology. This has led me to speculate that the ancients, who had always considered it important that sacrifices be remembered and recorded (*Iliad*, 22.170ff.; *Odyssey*, 4.762ff.), at a certain point saw their temples as assemblages of the materials, including food, used in sacrifice. This vision—which may not have been established until the first century B.C. or so—imparted to temple ornament a sacred, indeed tabooed, nature. Every molding was determined by strict rules for size, placement, and shape. And, in the same way that nowadays we obey all sorts of incest, dietary, and other taboos long after the myths purporting to explain them have been forgotten, so in later centuries architects have continued the ritual complexities of classicism even after all consciousness of a sacrificial meaning has ebbed away. Similarly, we perpetuate the rules for the "common-practice" period (roughly from Bach through Gounod) in musical harmony; and when a trained composer breaks those rules, he knows he is doing so, and hence salutes their existence. When, in the same spirit, a postmodern architect designs an ironically playful Palladian or Serlian window, we can only recognize it as such because we know, or at least sense, the rules for designing a serious and elegant Palladian window.

Most of the meanings and associations that go to make up these architectural rules come to us from Vitruvius, the first-century, Greek-trained Roman author of the only surviving classical treatise on architecture.[2] Esteemed by Renaissance architects who honored his treatise as a unique survival, Vitruvius has had a bad press in the last hundred years or so. His reputation shrank in modern times as more was learned about actual Greek and Roman building. It was found that he ignored important buildings of his own time and misdescribed ones he had not seen. His knowledge of the sixty-odd Greek architectural treatises that he mentions or paraphrases, all of them now lost, seems secondhand, and his own language is often confusing.[3]

These charges are not false. Yet Vitruvius had one immense advantage lacking to us: he lived in, was steeped in, an architectural sensibility that has since vanished. For all his narrowness and bias, he had at least seen buildings and books, had encountered architectural ideas, about which we know nothing except what he tells us. This is particularly true of his Greek culture. For though he is so often called Roman and linked to Augustus, Vitruvius was trained in a Hellenistic tradition carried on in the name of Hermogenes.[4] Nor does he cease to remind us that his culture is Greek. Words like *graece* and *Graecia* appear at least five times more often in his text than do *romanus* and *Roma*. Vitruvius's Greekness, and that of the contemporaneous Latin-language visual culture generally, will be my warrant for using Greek and Roman citations more or less interchangeably.

By the same token, though a few of my other authorities date from earlier times, most of them, whether they wrote in Greek or Latin, were Grecophile citizens of the Roman world: Philostratus, Callistratus, Strabo, Pliny, Plutarch, Lucian, Pausanias. They range in date from less than 100 B.C. through the third century A.D., mostly clustering around Vitruvius's own period. For this reason we may assume that the interpretation I here recover dates from this period (though that is not to deny that it may have existed earlier). Thus in the following pages I am not trying to establish how the orders really did come about. And I cannot even present this Hellenistic explanation, so to speak, as being particularly truthful. I examine the myth for its own sake, and also because it was taken seriously by some of the greatest architects of the Renaissance. That, in my view, gives it interest enough, and even fascination.

My method will be to unpack certain terms and passages from Vitruvius, and from other texts, so as to get out a fuller range of the meanings, associations, and images that lurk inside the words.

Vitruvius himself comments on this problem: "The terms necessarily devised for the special needs of architecture strike readers as obscure and outlandish. They are not obvious in themselves nor of common usage. Therefore as I introduce expressions from this jargon in enumerating the parts of a building, I shall give brief explanations, so as to fix them in memory" (5 Pref. 2). It is an admirable aim that unfortunately he does not carry out except here and there. I shall seek to supply these missing explanations, adding to them anything further that a modern reader might require.

For example: words like "Doric" and "echinus" carried very different associations in Vitruvius's time than they do now. Greek culture, moreover, encouraged the playing of associational games with words. Plato was fond of it. "Artemis," he has Socrates say, "appears to get her name from her healthy (ἀϱταμές) and well-ordered nature, and her love of virginity; or perhaps he who named her meant that she is learned in virtue (ἀϱετή), or, possibly, too, that she hates the sexual intercourse (ἄϱτον μισεῖ) of man and woman."[5] In the century following Vitruvius's, Clement of Alexandria claimed that all the gods' names were such tropes (*Protrepticon*, 2.24, 5.56). In the same spirit, in Apollodorus (*Library*, 2.4.5) Taphius names the people of his colony Teleboans because he had traveled far, τελοῦ ἔβη, from his native land. And the chorus in Euripides's *Iphigenia in Aulis* laments that immoderate ἔϱως, love, leads to ἔϱις, discord or jealousy (586ff.).

This sort of verbal play is called trope. The *Oxford English Dictionary* defines a trope as a word or phrase used in a sense other than that which is proper to it. But that is not the whole story. In Latin a *tropus* is a figure of speech, a simile, metaphor, catachresis, or the like.[6] Trope dwells in the world of puns, homonyms, and associations. It is playful and poetic, not scientific, and it is often etymologically incorrect. But it is unquestionably the way the ancients, including Vitruvius and his contemporaries, thought about words.

One thing that trope does is to link, through the pun or homonym, objects that otherwise seem to have little to do with each other. Some feel that this is a constant in human nature. Freud claims that, deep down, many minds will not "accept the similarity between two words as having no meaning; they consistently assume that if two things are called by similar-sounding names this must imply the existence of some deep-lying point of agreement between them."[7] Lévi-Strauss asserts that in the development of civilization trope preceded practical communication. He quotes Rousseau: "As emotions were the first motives that induced man to speak, his first utterances were tropes. Figurative language was the first to be born. At the beginning, only poetry was spoken."[8] Lévi-Strauss might better have quoted Vico, who, forty years before Rousseau, and building on the Renaissance emblematic tradition, founded his *scienza nuova* on the idea that the names of gods, goddesses, and heroes were, in Socrates's sense, tropes of social, political, economic, and religious changes in ancient societies. The myth about Orpheus, for example, whose lyre charms beasts, actually records the moment when law was first introduced into the society that invented that myth. After explaining that words for law are derived from words for tendons, that is, the sinews of the body politic, Vico continues, "and that nerve, or cord, or force that formed Orpheus's lyre" became "the union of the cords and powers of the fathers, whence derived public powers." Vico is here building on tropes of *corda,* which means tendon or sinew, lyre string, and also the musical chords those strings sound when played. The musical harmony of Orpheus's lyre introduces social harmony, in turn, for the earliest laws were poems (for example, the *Iliad* and the *Odyssey*), which taught the Greeks about the deeds of their ancestors and the edicts of their gods. Thus law and morality were first conceived of as a body of ancestral edicts preserved in works of art. By the same token, the beasts Orpheus charmed are not real beasts but lawful mankind's barbarian ancestors, who lived before the first laws were chanted.[9] Such is the analytic power of trope.

For an example more central to architecture, let us look at the tropes of a common feature of Doric, and of some Ionic, capitals. The ἐχῖνος, echinus, is the rounded shape forming part of the col-

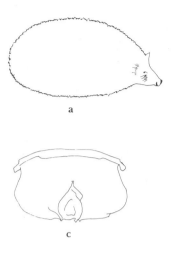
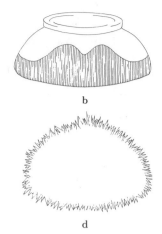

1
Drawings of ἐχῖνοι:
a. hedgehog; *b.* wide-
mouthed jar; *c.* neck
vertebra; *d.* sea urchin.

umn capital or "head" (Vitruvius, 4.3.4, 4.7.3). But ἐχῖνος means many other things: sea urchin, wide-mouthed jar, a vase for secret evidence, the shells of various plants and animals, a neck vertebra, the stomach of a ruminant, the pointed ends of a drilling bit, a plant, and a kind of cake. Thus Lucian writes, "They avoided taking hold of him as if he were an *echinus,* fearing his *acanthuses*" (*Bis Accusatus,* 34.15). To us this sounds like someone talking about an architectural capital; but acanthuses are also prickles, and in this case echinus means the prickly sea urchin.

All this seems to make "echinus" one of the words with several unconnected meanings of which Freud spoke. But the fact is that several of these objects involve similar compound curves broken up into spines or projections. In figure 1 I have drawn the hedgehog, the jar, the vertebra, and the sea urchin. (I have not found ancient images or descriptions of the profiles of the shells, the cake, and the bit. But they could be similar, as would be the ruminant's stomach.) In figure 2 I show profiles of the echini of a number of Greek Doric capitals. Note that all the capitals have necking

6

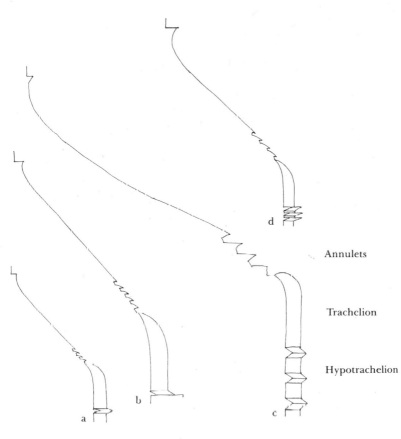

Annulets

Trachelion

Hypotrachelion

2
Profiles of four echini
from Greek Doric temples:
a. Aphaia, Aegina;
b. Neptune, Paestum;
c. Apollo, Delos; d. Partho
non, Athens. After Sir
Banister Fletcher, A History
of Architecture on the
Comparative Method, 1896.

3
Doric capital with painted
ornament. From Carl
Boetticher, *Die Tektonik der
Hellenen,* 1852.

grooves that give a silhouette of a compound curve articulated into a spiked pattern like that shown in the objects in figure 1.[10]

There is another way, aside from the silhouettes of the necking bands, in which Doric echini can be likened to spine-covered, gently curved shapes. Klaus Herrmann has recently published a study of painted Greek Doric capitals[11] which shows that all kinds of serrated, thorned, and spike-leaved decorations were carved or painted on the echinus's S-curved surface. He illustrates examples from Corfu, Sparta, Paestum, Mantinea, and other sites. Herrmann's finds buttress the suppositions of earlier scholars like Carl Boetticher, who claimed on the basis of literary evidence that Doric echini were frequently painted with friezes of spiny leaves (figure 3).

The word also has a mythological side. Echidna is the mother of the Lernian hydra and her lower body is that of the sharp-scaled viper. The *canis echidneus* is the three-headed dog, Cerberus (hence in Latin a thing that is *echarnatus* is bristly); and Echion was a hero who sprang from dragon's teeth. So the mythical tropes of "echinus" suggest apotropaic (pun intended) bristly things that will frighten off those who would break their taboos.

It is interesting, by the way, that trope itself, the word and the thing, is linked to a type of sacrifice made in ancient warfare. Since I will be dealing with architecture as a trope of sacrifice, the method and theme of this book are in themselves tropes. In Greek, τρόπος means style, turn, twist, hence the twisting of words. It is also connected with "trophy"—for trophies were originally erected at the point on the battlefield where the tide turned, ἔτρεψε, against the losers. (Indeed the word in Greek is commonly a verb, which warrants my using it as a verb in English.) Trophies, that is to say manikins formed of the arms, weapons, and helmets of the slain enemy, were set up to appease their shades and to prevent the gods from punishing the victors who had killed them. Their deaths were thus "turned," troped, from murders into sacrifices. Trophies were frequently used in architecture; and in chapter 3 we shall explore the connections between tropes, trophies, and temples.

In the following chapters I shall outline Greek sacrificial practices and the ways in which the names of objects used in animal and other kinds of ritual sacrifice were applied to ornaments (chapter 2). I shall look at a Greek temple that seems to have been consciously preserved in its primitive aspect into historical periods, and then at Vitruvius's stories of the invention of the Doric, Ionic, and Corinthian orders (chapter 3). Next, I shall analyze the tales of the caryatid and Persian porticoes as variants of these stories (chapter 4). By analyzing, as tropes, the key words in these tales, we will find that they describe the orders as records of sacrifice.

So much for that period in history during which, according to my theory, the connection between sacrifice and ornament was recognized because it was a part of everyday speech. The second part of the book deals with another great period of classicism in Western architecture, the Italian Renaissance. Here we find, in revived form, this same consciousness. And here too, particularly, I do not attempt complete coverage but make limited *sondages*. Two important architectural theorists, Francesco di Giorgio and Cesare Cesariano, are germane. And in different ways Raphael and Michelangelo preserved elements of the connection, which sheds new light on some of their greatest achievements: Raphael's *Disputà* and Michelangelo's tomb of Julius II and Medici Chapel (chapter 5). Knowledge of the connection is also traceable in handbooks: Hugues Sambin's book on termini (1572) maps the process by which humans emerge from stones, turn fully human, and then become gods, each stage, once again, being marked by sacrifices (chapter 6).

2

Architecture and Sacrifice

Sacred Trees

We have seen that both echini and acanthuses are or can be vegetal forms. Placed as they are at the summits of classical columns, they suggest the foliage of trees. And long before there were temples, the Greeks worshiped their gods in sacred groves or fields. Trees, rocks, mountains, and other natural objects contained divinities and were the objects or vessels of religious sacrifice. Indeed, says Carl Boetticher (still after more than a century the authority on the subject), "trees were the first temples."[1] He takes the claim from Pliny.[2]

There is even evidence that sacred trees could be holier than the altars that served them.[3] Each god and goddess had a special tree—the oak of Zeus, the myrtle of Aphrodite, the laurel of Apollo—which was also thought of as an image of its god. Thus Aphrodite's tree, or rather shrub, the myrtle, portrayed her,[4] and Pelops carved a statue of the goddess *from* a myrtle.[5] Conversely, in historic times the greatest statues ever made of Aphrodite, those by Praxiteles, now lost, were hailed as holy trees.[6]

The Greek art we know today is full of sacred trees. We see sacrifices being made before them, temples built around and within them, and gods and goddesses appearing in their branches. In a relief of Amphion and Zethos in the Palazzo Spada, Rome, a statue of Artemis stands before a sacred tree around which a temple has been constructed. Its columns are bound with a garland or banderole and *litui* or sacred staves; the skull of a sacrificed ox, a bucranium, decorates its entablature; and a garland, probably used in the sacrifice, hangs above the statue's head. The foreground is occupied by votaries, one bringing a lyre (figure 4). In another of

4
Tree aedicule of Artemis.
From Carl Boetticher, *Der Baumkultus der Hellenen*, 1856.

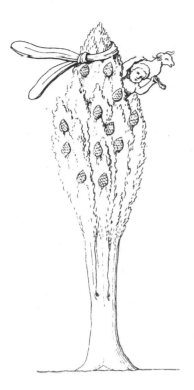

5
Sacred tree. From Carl
Boetticher, *Der Baumkultus
der Hellenen*, 1856.

Boetticher's illustrations we see a sacred cypress tree, bound with a garland and sprouting a divinity who shoulders a sacrificial lamb (figure 5).[7] Meanwhile the scholiast of Aristophanes tells us that the olive tree was Athena's temple, and her image, before there were such things as architectural temples or sculptured images.[8] Plutarch says the Romans had similar sacred trees (*Numa*, 8). Even after architectural temples came into existence, sacred trees remained. No temple was dedicated, says Boetticher, unless there was a holy tree associated with it.[9] More mockingly, Lucian records how the Greeks started their religion by fencing off groves of trees; only later did they erect temples and images (*On Sacrifices*, 10.01).

Such trees, or groups of trees, were often decorated with the gear and materials used in sacrifice and with the victims' remains: bones, horns, urns, lamps, fruit and vegetable relics, flowers, and weapons.[10] Vase paintings show how garlands, votive tablets, pearl strings or astragals, cymbals, crowns, drums or tympana, Bacchus masks, spears, skulls, and other sacrificial paraphernalia were arranged in the trees and suspended above the altars at their roots.[11]

Trees were often trimmed into the shape of primitive columns; indeed Vitruvius claims that the first columns *were* trees, or at least upright forked props tied together by horizontal branches (2.1.3). The notion that columns originated in the trimmed trunks of trees persisted into the Renaissance, as Francesco di Giorgio's *Trattato* shows us (figure 6).

And there is an element of truth in Vitruvius's assertion about columns deriving from trees. The first Greek temples, we know from archaeology, were indeed built of solid wooden columns,[12] and any such wooden temple column would in a sense be a sacred tree or tree trunk, especially since columns, like trees, had from prehistory been worshiped as the abodes or images of gods.[13] According to Pausanias, the first temple to Apollo at Delphi was a hut made of laurel trees.[14] And Apollodorus describes, at Elis, the wooden column of Oenomaos, a hero of Pindar's first Olympian ode. This was a relic of Oenomaos's house, where Pelops, a god-king and a founder of Athens, revered the severed heads of his unsuccessful rivals for the hand of Oenomaos's daughter.[15] It was Oenomaos who had slain them, and I suppose one might think of the decorative display of their heads over a door as their transformation into trophies. This in turn might have transformed the murders into sacrifices. We do not know that the wooden pillar was part of the trophy, though that is of course possible. In any event this historic column was re-erected near the sanctuary of Zeus and an aedicule was built around it. There it functioned as a sacred tree-column.

Sacrifice

Let us now take a look at the act of sacrifice as performed, for example, before these sacred trees or before the temples that later supplemented them. I paraphrase Walter Burkert's description of a typical sacrifice to an Olympic god (bracketed passages are my own insertions).[16]

6
Francesco di Giorgio,
Column and tree. From
the Saluzziano Codex,
Biblioteca Reale, Turin,
folio 15r.

The participants bathe and dress themselves in special clothes and ornaments, including wreaths. They then go singing in procession to the place of sacrifice. They are led by a girl called a canephoros carrying a basket of grain on her head. An animal victim accompanies the procession. [He is led by a rope or halter, and his feet are probably hobbled.] He too is decorated with wreaths, and his horns, if he has them, are gilded. The music of a flute is heard. The event itself takes place before an altar stone, if possible very ancient. [The longer it has been in use, the more blood it has absorbed, the more relics of earlier sacrifices it displays, the holier it is.] A fire now burns on it, a censer smokes, and there is a jug of water nearby. The participants draw a circle around themselves in the earth. The area enclosed becomes a sacred precinct. The basket and waterjug are carried round it to reaffirm the consecration. All wash their hands, and the victim is sprinkled. He is perceived as willing, even anxious, to be sacrificed and to this end is forced to nod his head.

Raw barley grains are taken from the canephoros's basket and flung by the sacrificers over the animal, the altar, and the earth. Silent and spoken prayers follow. But now the basket reveals its more sinister contents, which had been hidden by the grain: the sacrificial knife. The leader of the ritual, the priest or ἱερεύς, steps forward and takes it. He cuts a lock of hair from the animal's brow and throws it into the fire. Then he slits the victim's throat. As he does so the women scream, ὀλολυγέ, a shout of terror, acknowledging that the god has come into their presence. The beast's blood, which is considered precious, must not reach the ground but must drain through the altar into conduits and pits beneath. The animal is then carefully carved up, part by part, the head, thighs, feet, joints, and horns being separated in accordance with powerful taboos. The heart, sometimes still beating, is placed on the altar. A seer interprets the liver: it is thus that the god makes known his message. Then certain parts, the σπλάγχνα, are roasted and eaten. The rest is preserved [Pausanias, 2.40.5]. The bones are consecrated and placed on or over the altar, especially the thighbones, μηρία, which are chopped into parts and wrapped in fat.

Next, the bones and skull are arranged on the altar so as to suggest the general outline of the beast. To complete the effigy the animal's skin is draped over them. Later, the bones, skull, and horns are bleached in the fire and preserved as relics. These were thought to contain divine life-giving fluids that the fire released among the congregation.[17] When the blood has ceased to drain into the fire, offerings of wine, honey, vegetables, flowers, fruit, and cakes are cast onto the blaze. With the final feast, marked by revelry and sometimes debauchery, the sacrifice is over.

Greek sacrifice thus involved the deconstruction and reconstruction of the victim's body. This is not surprising. There is no shortage of evidence as to the importance in classical religion of body parts, and myth is full of ritual dismemberments. The most famous are those of the Bacchae, the women who, filled with drunken rage—that is, with the presence of Dionysus—took apart the corpses of their victims.[18] The stories of Phrixus, Itys, Procne, Orpheus, and of Dionysus himself, butchered and cooked by the Titans, are other cases in point. In these dismemberments, as in sacrifice, there was often a subsequent reconstruction. "Time and again in myth," writes Burkert, "the remnants of a victim torn apart are collected, deposited, brought back to life."[19] Let us note that many of these myths about reconstructed victims are foundation myths for religious rituals; in other words, they are a precondition for the erection of temples.

But Greek sacrifice could also involve the construction, or reconstruction, of the god himself as he presided over his offerings.

7
Lenaia vase, c. 450 B.C.
Museum of Fine Arts,
Boston. Anonymous gift.

Such scenes appear frequently in art, for example, on the Lenaia vases used in the Dionysus cult (figure 7). I illustrate an Attic red-figure stamnos by the Villa Giulia painter, c. 450 B.C., depicting two worshipers in front of the Dionysus image. Before the image is a table of offerings with two large wine jugs and piled high with fruit. The image proper consists of a shaft dressed in a pleated chiton and topped with a bearded mask. Above this is a crown and symmetrical spray of foliage. The likeness to a column with flutes and capital is striking.

Hunting was also a form of sacrifice, as here again the killer did penance for his deed, identified with his victim, and attempted to reconstruct him. "Wishing to save the animal from complete destruction and to regenerate symbolically his future source of food," writes one authority on prehistoric Greek hunting, "the hunter removed and treated its internal organs in special ways and buried or preserved certain of its bones, often reconstituting them in a particular pattern that, supplemented by the addition of small pieces of meat from other limbs, suggested the regeneration of the whole beast."[20] Similarly, in historic times Greek hunters hung the skulls of their prey on stakes and draped these stakes in the animals' skins.

Why should dismembered victims be reconstructed? It is generally agreed that the animal victims were later substitutes for another sort of victim, though there is less agreement as to what that other sort was. Burkert states one of the most popular views when he says sacrifices were much later reenactments of primal ritual murders in which a god-king was killed and consumed.[21] But whether or not animal sacrifices reenacted human ones, there clearly was the sense among the worshipers that blood sacrifice was a crime of some sort. Priests who sacrificed animals could be tried for doing so even when, presumably, they had simply fulfilled their religious duties.[22] Sometimes even the murder weapon itself was convicted.[23] This explains why an Early Christian convert from paganism like Clement of Alexandria could claim that pagan religion consisted of "disguised murders and burials" (*Protrepticon*, 2.16). The reconstitution of the victim on the altar could be a sort of denial that it had ever been killed, or better still could suggest that, thus reconstituted and set in a holy place, it was reborn as an immortal. Its translation from living being into image was a warrant of divinity, a memorial to the fact that its body had once held the god's soul.[24]

Whether or not it represented a killed king, the victim was the unquestioned vessel of the god.[25] When the victim's own spirit departed, the god filled up the victim's skin, whether it was an animal, plant, fruit, flower, or vegetable or for that matter coins, blood, or a sword or a helmet—for all these too could be "victims" in the sense that they were common offerings to the gods. Clement of Alexandria castigated the Greeks for not only offering, but worshiping, specially shaped cakes, balls of salt, pomegranates, fig branches, fennel stalks, ivy leaves, and poppies (*Protrepticon*, 2.19).

Whatever form the victim or offering took, once it was ἔνθεος, full of the god, according to Hubert and Mauss, the divinity became too immense, too terrible, to be contained. It was necessary to break apart the offering. Yet even after death—perhaps especially after it—the animal's carcass, the god's container, was steeped in his presence. This is why the worshipers ate parts of it: the act was not just feasting, but communion. The worshipers' own bodies combined with parts of the victim's to express the fact that the god had entered them. The victim's body parts were in fact "reconstructed," now in a different way, by uniting the bodies of the worshipers.

To the ancients the limbs and organs of the body were felt to be the seats of different aspects of the personality. Heads, eyes, tongues, ears, fingers, thighs, and the like were thought to be sacred to the soul, to the temper, to one's human worth and *virtù*. (The title of R. B. Onians's great book, on which I here rely, makes the point: *The Origins of European Thought about the Body, the Mind, the Soul, the World, Time, and Fate*). So even the uneaten σπλάγχνα, as I will call them—bones, skin, and the like[26]—underwent a type of reconstruction. They were arranged in rows on tables of offering, set out on the tops of walls, or made into pendants and hung on ὀβελοί, obelisks,[27] a word that basically means spit or skewer for meat. Whether rearranged on an altar or eaten by the congregation, the victim's remains were clearly too holy to be thrown away or ignored.

The sensibility surrounding funeral practice is similar. The death of a human being, like that of an animal, was or could be sacrificial. Once again the bones were considered significant, taboo. The purpose of cremation was to obtain them quickly. "The most sacred duty for the next-of-kin," writes Burkert, "is to gather the bones (ὀστολογεῖν, *ossa legere*) from the ashes of the pyre." Here again the notion of a divine meal is present, though it is not the worshiper but the fire—that is, the god—which "eats" the corpse. When the fire finishes its meal, the bones and ashes are united in an urn. "This act is at once a joining together and a foundation, as in the Latin word *condere*."[28] Thus an urn with its contents is a concretion or reconstruction of the dead person within it. It is one more form of preserved and recorded sacrifice.

Warfare also had its kinship to sacrifice and to funeral practices, as well as to hunting, of course. Burkert even claims that war was "one great sacrificial action."[29] If a friendly god could occupy a sacrifical animal, a hostile one could occupy the body of an enemy soldier. And that too resulted in σπλάγχνα that had to be cherished and displayed. "Argos hung high on its temples the many spoils of the barbarians," says the farmer in the prologue to *Electra* (6ff.), referring not to the soldiers' bodies but to their armor and weapons. I suppose that when Pelops worshiped trophies that really were body parts, the suspended heads of his matrimonial rivals, he was doing something similar. The heads were holy, the spoils of his father-in-law's triumph. Pelops honored himself by honoring them, and by honoring them also kept their ghosts at bay. Similarly, military *exuviae* (spoils) had to be honored so that the spirits of the dead would not trouble the victors (*Aeneid*, 11.5ff., 11.83ff.). Trophies, like sacrificial victims, also involved reconstruction. The trophies of goats sacrificed before battle were called αἰγίδες, aegises, and were said to be representations of Athena with her helmet and shield.[30]

Sacrificial Terminology in Architecture

If we put all this together we can see the temple as a grove of
sacred trees decorated with battle or hunting trophies, or decked
out like an altar, with reconstructed sacrifices. Rows of teeth, garlands, horns, bones, weapons, and other things taken from victims
figure in such displays, as do flowers, fruit, and the like. In a similar spirit Clement of Alexandria implies that temple statues were
made out of these sacrificial materials (*Protrepticon*, 4.48).

The names for the different elements of a temple's architectural
order—the decorations of base, shaft, capital, architrave, frieze,
cornice, and pediment—bear this out.

Some forms of ornament, and their names, seem derived from
the process of bringing the victim to the altar. A column base,
βάσις, is first of all a foot, but the word also means footwork—
stepping and rhythmic movement. Bogdan Rutkowski is only the
most recent of a line of scholars who have emphasized the importance of dance rituals that took place before temples;[31] and the
dancing personage may be seen, furthermore, as a victim, for victims were supposed to be delighted at having been chosen. We
have also noted the correspondence between hunting and sacrifice,
especially animal sacrifice, and that the victim's feet were tied much
as a hunter ties up his game. Note too that Baroque statue-columns
often have bound feet (figures 74, 75). Furthermore, a cavetto
molding, common in column bases, gets its name from heavy rope,
and a torus or σπεῖρα is also a rope, one that is twisted or slung.
And a column base composed of toruses and cavetti often does
resemble a set of tautened ropes (figure 8). All these elements
come together in statue-columns with feet bound by what appear
to be toruses and cavetti (figure 70, bottom, second from left).

Another aspect of the column base is its rich endowment of horizontal shadows. The molding that achieves them is the *scotia*. This
is a fairly significant word in Greek, for Σκοτία is the name of the
goddess of darkness and underworld things.[32] Darkness or shadow
was perceived by the ancients not as the mere absence of light but
as a palpable substance, a vapor that was dark because it was dense

8
Richard Morris Hunt and
Richard Howland Hunt,
Torus or rope moldings,
facade of the Metropolitan
Museum of Art, New York,
1895–1902.

with the tiny mote-like souls of the dead.[33] So if we look again at the shadows cast by a scotia molding, we are to see them as thick with souls (figure 9). Apophysis, ἀπόφυσις, the hollow curve between a column's base and shaft, is taken from the word for part of a bone or blood vessel; and the juncture in a column between the flute and the arris or edge that separates the flutes does emphasize the flutes' quality as hollow bony channels or conduits (figure 9).[34]

Other parts of the column have human content as well. For example, the vertical fillets created by carving flutes in a column are called ῥάβδοι, rods, staves, or wands, a word used also for the shafts of spears. Allan Greenberg's stopped flutes in figure 10, which take the form of gilded shafts, make the point particularly well. These suggest not only the trophies of the hunt and war, but the bunched shafts used in constructing Dionysus images. And yet we know from Vitruvius (4.1.7) that flutes were also felt to resemble the folds in a chiton.[35] Meanwhile the trachelion and hypotrachelion come from τράχελος, throat; and in the examples in figure 2 the throat shape and placement are clearly preserved.

The most human and also the most sacrificial part of a column is the capital (κεφάλιον, κεφαλίς, head). It is of course the column's head, the head of the personage whose feet, form, and throat stand below; and here again we come to the presence of souls, for the heads of humans, animals, and even plants (i.e., their blossoms) were thought to contain their spiritual essences.[36] But just as a trophy consists of the warrior's outer teguments—breastplate, helmet, spear, etc.—so the column head really consists of headdresses, head ornaments. We noted earlier that the Doric capital is formed of an echinus carved or decorated with spiny leaves, in other words a garland of a type commonly worn around the head. Similarly, the capital of an anta was called the ἐπίκρανον, which also means a kerchief.[37] Ionic and Corinthian capitals have head garlands, including blossoms, and also hair and horns (figures 11, 12). We have noted that the heads, or skulls, of victims were displayed on shrines[38] and that the remains to which Pelops sacrificed were the exhibited heads of his rivals in love. It is quite possible, as I have

9
Thomas Hastings with
Everett V. Meeks,
Corinthian column base
with scotia moldings,
Colonnade, Yale
University, 1927. Above is
the apophysis.

10
Allan Greenberg,
Fireplace, Secretary's
study, Department of
State, Washington, D.C.,
1984–85. (Photo. Richard
Cheek)

11
Hiss and Weekes, Ionic
capital, Byers Hall, Yale
University, 1902. The
fascias are the three
horizontal bands above the
capitals.

12
Ithiel Town, Capital, Mary
Prichard house, New
Haven, 1836.

13
McKim, Mead and White,
Anthemions with faces,
Metropolitan Museum of
Art, New York, 1906.

suggested, that these heads adorned the tops of wooden columns,
though Apollodorus says they were placed over a door (*Epitome*,
2.5), presumably like acroteria in the form of anthemions, which
so frequently do contains heads (figure 13). The Corinthian capital
illustrated in figure 12 is the very image of horns emerging from
fronded hair; indeed, the acanthus leaves look more like hair than
foliage. I am reminded of a poem in the *Anacreontea* (17.6ff.):
"Twisting locks curling against each other and wanting anything
but flatness." Similarly the hair we see coiled in Ionic capitals (figure 11; Vitruvius 4.1.7) can be likened to the specially prepared
coils of hair, πλόκαμοι, offered in sacrifices (Callimachus, *Aetia*,
110.47). Meanwhile the pulvinus, the coiled side of an Ionic volute,
is the προσκεφάλαιον, "a head protector." In the example in figure
14, the tightly rolled hair at the sides of the "head," expressed by
curling tendrils and leaves and, below, by hirsute palmettes, is
wrapped in a lappeted band. But in Greek κόμη means either hair
or foliage.

14
Gordon, Tracy, and
Swartwout, Pulvinus of an
Ionic capital, Connecticut
Savings Bank, New Haven,
1906. The echinus is the
bulging egg-and-dart
molding on the left.

The volutes of the Ionic and Corinthian capitals also resemble horns, those omnipresent sacrifical objects. Horns were gilded for sacrifice, as if precious. And indeed they were. They contained a soul-like substance, psyche, ψυχή, the life power.[39] Horn head-dresses were worn by Cypriote priests;[40] and in Minoan times horns, real or sculptured, presided over altars and sanctuaries (as they did in many other ancient religions, as at Çatal Hüyük). Vincent Scully has shown how sacred horned mountains functioned as visual anchors in the siting of Greek temples.[41] Some divinities were horned: Artemis was called Ταυροπόλος, bull-crowned, by Euripides (*Iphigenia in Taurica*, 1456). In legend, horns and horned gods were particularly associated with the Dorians, who, according to Vitruvius (4.1), founded the Doric and Ionic orders.[42] Coiled horns were especially prized. We get the word "helix" from them (used by Anacreon to describe his boyfriend's hair), and ἐλιξόκερως means twisted-horned. ἕλικαι are any sort of wreathed or spiralled thing, including vine tendrils, arm bracelets, and hair, as well as volutes on column capitals. Related to this is the caulicolus of the Corinthian capital, the tight spiral curl at the upper corners (figure 12). This is a καυλεῖον, which means both the stalk of a plant and a hunter's crook-headed staff, which brings up once again the theme of hunting. Ithiel Town, no doubt aware of none of this but literally copying an antique precedent, the capitals of the Choregic Monument of Lysicrates in Athens, made his leaves hairlike and curly, filled with tight tendrils and combed into curving locks.

Above the columns is the broad expanse of the entablature. The very word, though English, not Greek or Latin (those languages use *epistylium*, meaning the thing on top of columns), suggests that it could be thought of as a table. And it comes from the Latin *tabulatum*, which means both table and tablet. It can thus be compared to the tables of offerings outside temples, on which flowers, fruit, vegetables, and other "victims" were arranged.

In the Doric order the entablature is divided into triglyphs and metopes. If the head was by all odds the most important part of the body, the knee, the thighbone or femur, and hair were also sacred. Their life-giving fluids were of the greatest importance.[43] The victim's thighbones were displayed to certify that a god had actually descended upon an altar.[44] Homer habitually refers to sacrifices as the offering of μηροί, thighs; and so let us note that the three uprights in a triglyph are called by this name. The same is true in Latin: *femores*. (In Greek, furthermore, the word is close to the word for share or offering, which would thus trope the body part received in communion.) Since "glyph" means something carved or chopped off, a tri-glyph is or can be a thighbone chopped into three. (τρίγλυφος means thrice-cloven.) We saw, too, that the thighbones were wrapped in a layer of fat. In the same way the μηροί of the triglyph are wrapped in their upper and lower διαζώματα, a word that means girdles, bindings, and layers as well as the friezes in Ionic and Corinthian architecture. Another word that may have been used is κανών, which means rod or bar. These correspond to the Latin *regulae*, rules or rulers, which is the word for the lower horizontal bar (figure 15) in a Doric triglyph. We can even see the σταγῶνες, *guttae*, drops, beneath as drops draining from the thighbones (figure 16). These drops represent the sacred fluids that were carefully drained into the altar, or they can be read as memorials of the different aspergings done by the priest in sacrifice.[45] The triglyphs illustrated in figure 15 were designed by Allan Greenberg, who assures me that he had no idea such meanings lay within the forms, or even the names of the forms, he was working with. But the essential device of three upright bones wrapped top and bottom with strands of dripping fat is clearly readable. Like Ithiel Town before him, Greenberg unconsciously preserved the meaning of the forms simply by copying precedent.

The word μετόπη or μετόπιον, metope (the area between the triglyphs in a Doric frieze), is usually derived from μεθ' ὀπαῖς, between holes, and thus means the panel between the interstices between beam ends. This may be correct etymologically, but let us not forget the word μέτωπον, forehead or front, which is also the space between the eyes, the brow. Thus μετωπηδόν means front foremost, and there is a host of derivatives referring to headwear and kerchiefs. So the metope is tinged with tropes of "head" as well

15
Allan Greenberg, Dentils,
triglyphs, regulae, and
guttae, Reception rooms,
Department of State,
Washington, D.C., 1984–
85. (Photo: Richard
Cheek)

16
Hale and Rogers, Guttae
or drops, Edward S.
Harkness house, New
York, 1905.

as being the space between the displayed triglyphs. Once more, that is, we have the notion that important body parts decorate the upper regions of a classical building.

The moldings of these upper regions have the sacrificial *sfumatura* we see in so much of the rest of this terminology. One of the most common moldings is the cyma, an S-curve that is either *recta* or *reversa* depending on the position of the curve (figure 17).[46] κύματα are basically waves, and the shape of the molding suggests a wave; but we cannot set aside the basic role of moldings, which is to drain the facade. In this sense we may think of a "wave" of rainwater, for example, washing down the front of the frieze beneath the cyma.[47]

A more prominent molding is what we call egg-and-dart or tongue-and-dart (figure 18). Eggs were much used and much prized in temple precincts. We see eggs and the doves that laid them featured in medallion portrayals of the shrine at Paphos (figure 25). This no doubt reflects the fact that eggs laid by the innumerable birds belonging to temples, ranging from hens to turtledoves, were sold as souvenirs.[48] On altars eggs were carved in ᾠοθεσία or decorative rows paralleling other kinds of molding. Aristeas Judaeus describes the egg-and-dart molding on an altar made for the temple at Jerusalem as a gift from Ptolemy Philadelphus.[49] He uses the phrase ὁμοίως κατὰ τήν τῆς ᾠοθεσίας διασκευὴν κατεσκεύασατο, καὶ τὰ λοιπὰ τῆς ῥαβδώσεως καὶ διαγλυφῆς, which I take to be a description of the alternating open-shelled eggs and vertical rods (ῥάβδοι) that are one of the commonest Ionic moldings (figure 18). This, so far as I know, is the only description of such a molding to appear in classical Greek. And in that language a ῥάβδος can be several things—a rod or staff, a limed twig for catching birds, a whip, a line of verse, a streak on an animal's skin, and the flutes of a column[50]—but not a dart. Burkhardt Wesenberg meanwhile thinks that the ὄνυξες in an inscription connected with the Erechtheum in Athens may refer to such a molding.[51] ὄνυξ means several different things, chiefly claws. Thus if there were vertical rods between the eggs in Aristeas's molding, in that of the Erechtheum we would have a row of

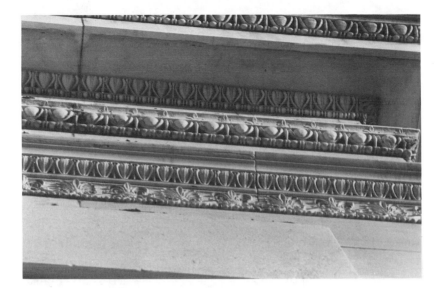

17
Gordon, Tracy, and
Swartwout, Cyma
moldings, Connecticut
Savings Bank, New Haven,
1906.

18
Gordon, Tracy, and
Swartwout, Egg-and-dart
molding, Connecticut
Savings Bank, New Haven,
1906.

eggs beneath a row of (bird) claws. And this three-pronged element (figures 17, 55) is as common in these moldings as are the rods. Thus it would be more proper to refer to "egg-and-claw" moldings—though the moldings on the Erechtheum, despite the claws in the inscription, are more like the eggs and darts in figure 18 than the eggs and claws in figure 55.

Eggs, like fruit, were common sacrifices.[52] They were a form of head, since they contained souls, either of birds[53] or of other beings, including humans. Sometimes the eggs in egg-and-claw moldings are shown with shells split open. This reveals the "soul," or yolk, κόκκος (figure 57). Nuts, berries, flowers, and egg yolks were also considered kinds of heads and called κόκκοι. More importantly, κοκύαι are ancestors, which brings up an aspect of these ornaments that will be investigated in the next two chapters.

Above and below the rows of eggs and claws across an entablature are the ταινία, or fascias, especially in the Ionic/Corinthian architrave (figure 11). The taenia, a binding like the moldings at the column's base, is in its primary meaning a head or breast band. Also to be found among these moldings is the astragal, ἀστραγάλος, which refers to a string of pearls or knucklebones, or to vertebrae (figure 19).[54] According to Clement of Alexandria (*Protrepticon*, 2.15), ἀστράγαλοι were used in religious services. Most astragal moldings do resemble stringings of bead-shaped bones or the like. Vertebrae appear again in the word σφόνδυλος, which also means column drum.[55]

Several of the forms we have looked at suggest food and eating—the eggs, fruit, vegetables, bones, and, quite possibly, the forms that control dripping and draining. In addition, caulicolae are sprouts of cabbage, and anthemions are camomile, another edible plant.[56] But nothing suggests eating more than teeth do—that is, dentils (figure 16). In Greek these rows of architectural teeth are ὀδοντοφόροι, a word that also refers to strings of teeth used to ornament horses. Tongues (*linguae*) and beaks (*rostra*) are other moldings that are juxtaposed with the many sorts of edibles that appear in Greek ornament.

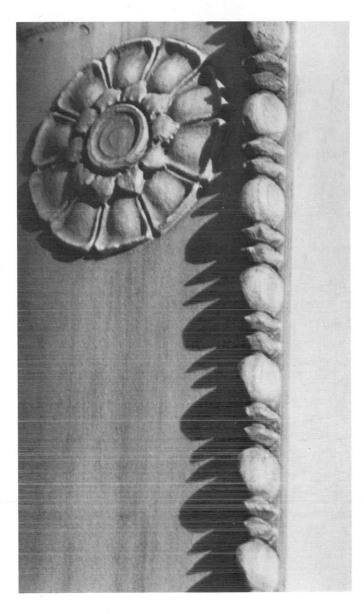

19
Gordon, Tracy, and
Swartwout, Astragal
(right), Connecticut
Savings Bank, New Haven,
1906.

Above the entablature rises the triangular pediment,[57] consisting of a tympanum enclosed by moldings (figure 20). Originally a tympanum was a structure of bones covered with animal skins and used as a drum: the same materials used, we note, to reconstruct victims on altars. And, though they were chiefly drums, tympana were also used as tables. Clement of Alexandria says of certain worshipers that they ἐκ τυμπάνου ἔφαγον, ate from a tympanum; that is, presumably they ate pieces of a sacrificed animal set out on the tympanum created from his remains or those of a predecessor (*Protrepticon*, 2.14). This reinforces our reading of the temple's upper part as a table. Moreover, if a tympanum is a reconstructed animal, the tympanum's central block is that animal's head, for this is the *columen* in Latin and in Greek the κορυφαῖον. More specifically, a κορυφαῖον is the head of a sacrificed animal—but also, interestingly, the upper rim of a hunting net (Xenophon, *Cynegeticus*, 10.2). One is here reminded of the enormous head of the Gorgon in the tympanum of the temple at Corfu (seventh/sixth century B.C.).

The cornice, crown, or *corona* than mainly comprises the molding surrounding the tympanum proclaims the subordination to it of everything below. Thus in Rome when a prisoner was taken he or she was said to be *sub corona*.[58] In Greek the corona is very different. It is called the γεῖσον, which means simply a coping, a projection or other border, even a hem. But the sense that the crown controls the things below it appears in other ways. The descending slopes of the corona are called the ἀετός, eagle. Pindar's thirteenth Olympian ode attributes the invention of the tympanum's raking cornice to Corinth and says the first "pair of eagle wings" was set up in a pediment possibly to subdue the violent actions of its sculptured horses[59] (which, as elements of the tympanum, represented the reconstituted victim). It is true that, as birds, eagles have little to do with sacrifice, unless one wants to count the stories of Prometheus, Ganymede, or the Roman *aquila sancta,* which is a military goddess (*Corpus Inscriptionum Latinarum,* 3.6224). The military standards of the Persians, as well as of the Romans, were called eagles, however (Xenophon, *Cyropedia,* 7.1.4). Hence an "eagle" adorning a temple might have trophaic value, like captured weap-

20
Allen and Williams, State
Circuit Court, New Haven,
1909.

ons. And above all the eagle was a bird of omen (*Iliad*, 8.247, 12.201; *Odyssey*, 2.146) and Zeus's favorite bird (Pindar, *Pythian*, 1.6). For all these reasons it is appropriate to top off a temple with an ἀετός.

Other terms not connected with the temple-front proper have comparable meanings. The word *ancones*, ἀγκῶνες, corbels, comes from a word that basically means elbows or any limb that bends or embraces. Vitruvius uses *ancones* eight times, but he also indicates the same architectural element with other words that refer to curved body parts. Thus in 4.6.4 he gives *parotides*, ear pieces, as a synonym for it. And in the example I give from Richard Morris Hunt, the ear shape is pronounced (figure 21). The three Michelangelesque guttae that hang from the lobe function as earrings.

I have mentioned the liquids and vapors in sacrificial remains and speculated that the guttae of the Doric triglyph may portray them. Similarly, in temple architecture many moldings and details are designed to allow for the runoff of water so that the points of the building will be kept dry. This is what guttae were supposed to do. They are small disks or cones and gather real drops, when it rains, so that they wash down the face of the structure rather than inside the masonry. The soffit of the cornice also usually contains guttae, arranged in panels. The curious entablature of one New York house, built for Edward S. Harkness, provides both types of guttae, but without triglyphs (figure 16).[60] Looking up at this soffit one sees the upper maw of a beast, lips drawn back, gums salivating, and a row of dentils. The water had to be extruded, just as soul, life-force, strength, sexual ability, and other god-given powers were conceived as fluids to be absorbed by, or removed from, the human body. Indeed αἰών, aeon, means both spinal marrow and destiny, perhaps with the idea that one's fate is bound up with this fluid. Temples sweat, as stone sweats, and they weep with rain, and the moldings and ornament channel those fluids exactly as their counterparts are channeled in sacrifices, where the altars are equipped with gratings and tubes for the flow and collection of blood, wine, honey, and other offered substances.

21
Richard Morris Hunt and
Richard Howland Hunt,
Ancones or corbels for a
lintel, Metropolitan
Museum of Art, New York,
1892–1902.

And not only altars. Robert Garland has shown that stone funeral stelai in Greece were anointed by the survivors of the deceased almost like living things. "Oiled, perfumed, decorated, crowned and fed, [the stele] was a focus of devotion and an object of adoration."[61] In Hyginus Gromaticus (1.141) we read: "They set stones vertically in solid earth . . . they decorated them with unguents, garlands, and clothing . . . they sprinkled them with blood and laid fruit and frankincense, beans and vines on them . . . and when the [god's] meal had been consumed by the fire they laid the smoking remains on the stones."[62] A more important stone would have been carved with replicas of these remains to immortalize the sacrifice made that day; with the ribbons and bands that tied it together; and with guttae, channels, and flutes to carry off the fluids.

One of the chief divinities in all this is Artemis. The shadow molding, for example, is called by her epithet, Scotia. And not only was she ταυροπόλος, bull-crowned, horned, but she was also a sacred slaughterer of animals. We shall see that Vitruvius makes her a key figure in the foundation of the "horned" Ionic order. Sacrifices to her, as might be expected, were specially rich in σπλάγχνα. Her most notorious rites were celebrated at Patras (Pausanias, 7.18.11ff.). A table of offerings or altar of dry, easily burnt wood was surrounded by a palisade of green wood that was relatively uninflammable. The sacrificers then assembled creatures that had been caught in a hunt in Artemis's honor, filling the platform with live game secured by nets, chains, and ropes so they could not escape. The priestesses then set fire to it. As the offerings were thus consumed by the fire, the celebrants danced around the altar in a circle.[63] Such sacrifices not only produced exuviae consisting of bird's beaks, skulls, teeth, bones, and the like, but also the nets, claws, and other implements with which the victims were caught and made fast to the altar. One of Artemis's most famous epithets was Δίκτυννα, the drawer of nets. She was Diana Dictynna to the Romans (Ovid, Metamorphoses, 2.441). And her cult preserved more than a hint of the aboriginal tree-temples, too, for we read in the Palatine Anthology and in Philostratus of her forest shrines made in the old style, of tree trunks, and festooned with relics and weapons of the hunt.[64]

Taboo and Detail

One way of characterizing sacred trees, their decorations, and of course sacrifice itself is to say these things are taboo—a paradoxical word that means both holy and unholy. Both Greek and Latin have words equivalent to "taboo"—ἄγος (expiation, but also pollution; also the holy and the damned) and *sacer* (sacred, but also detestable).[65] (French preserves the dual meaning in *sacré*, but there is no equivalent in English.[66]) Thus, writes Herodotus, "a curse fell upon them, ἄγος σφι ἐγένετο, which no amount of sacrifice could take away" (6.91). Similarly, in Sophocles's *Antigone* ἄγος on one occasion means pollution and on another freedom from pollution (256, 775).

Among the Romans, individuals, tribes, and cities could be *sacer*, again in the sense of being holy or damned or both at once. A human loved by a god is *sacer*, and so is a king.[67] One's soul and blood are *sacer*. In Rome the tribunes of the Roman plebs, aediles, and decemviral judges were *sacer*: whoever hurt a "sacrosanct" tribune sacrificed his possessions to Ceres and his head to Jupiter (Livy, 3.55). Ponticus is quoted as saying that a *homo sacer* is a man whom the community judges to be evil and who should be sacrificed. Yet, paradoxically, anyone worthy of sacrifice is worthy of the gods. Like Sophocles's ἄγη he "belongs" to them for the very reason that men disown him. The plural of *sacer*, *sacra*, is the commonest Latin word for sacrifices and religious festivals. So the word "sacrifice," *sacrificium*, might be translated as making taboo. Indeed, by means of tropes of ἄγος we can picture an entire sacrifice in these terms: ἄγος, is holy, taboo; the similar word ἀγός means leader, chief, or king. An ἀγών is a gathering, assembly, public contest, and place of contest, and ἄγρα refers to hunting and the slaughter of animals. The words (as tropes, I repeat, not as etymologically related expressions) paint the picture of a ruler or priest in a field celebrating a blood sacrifice before his people.

But taboo is not just a question of attraction and repulsion; the dangers and blessings involved are so powerful that the actions to be performed can only be approached with the most extreme ceremony. Let us note that the classical orders are similarly beset. This I believe is what Nietzsche meant when he described the "atmosphere of inexhaustible meaningfulness" that hung about ancient temples "like a magic veil . . . the basic feeling of uncanny sublimity, of sanctification by magic or the gods' nearness . . . the *dread* [that] was the prerequisite everywhere."

Temples were not only the settings of taboo,[68] they were also its objects. And so were other kinds of buildings. As Burkert remarks, "A house, a bridge, a dam, was only valid from the moment that a sacrificed life lay beneath it."[69] Thus, on occasion, the two kinds of taboos, those of the gods and those of the gods' temples, merge. One major type of taboo has to do with territorial or boundary sanctions. Columns mark out boundaries, property, and jurisdictions. In the *Fasti* (2.639ff.) Ovid hails the god Terminus, who frequently occupies human-headed stone stelai that have been set as boundary markers between fields. The adjacent property owners make sacrifices to Terminus and decorate his image with exuviae. Thus Terminus, who as we shall see also inhabits an important type of column, involves, indeed embodies, a territorial taboo.

The rules for the orders, as taboos, partake of the obsession with body parts that runs throughout pagan sacrifice. Vitruvius divides the human body into head, fingers, palms, and feet (3.1). These are then correlated with specific proportions or fractions, for example the δίμοιρος, two-thirds, and the πεντάμοιρος, five-sixths. Everything is distributed, located, and measured by applying formulas to the body parts or fractions. A molding is so many fingers thick, a column is spaced so many feet from its neighbor, and so on. The same would apply to the other numerical systems of feet, inches (i.e., thumbs), fingers, heads, hands, and the like, preached by other theorists. When the rules are broken, we feel the result is not so much solecism as blasphemy. Vitruvius's minuteness and admonitory tone give his text the quality of the endless dietary taboos in Deuteronomy 14 and Leviticus 11, or the long lists of prohibitions in some Orphic or Pythagorean sect.

If my thesis is correct that, at least to the Greek-speaking world in Vitruvius's age, a great deal of classical ornament represented the remains or trophies of sacrifice, such ornament would represent reconstitutions or reformations of the remains into images of the victims. The imagery is, moreover, polyvalent. Horns can double as hair, vegetables as staves, pleats in a chiton as bunches of spear shafts. That is unsurprising. For one thing it is the price of any sort of representation: the artist or craftsman is essentially portraying one thing with another. But I should also note that sacrifice is essentially the transformation of an animal into a god and then the further fusing of that animal-god with the worshipers. The relics of all these metamorphoses are then arrayed on altars, tables of offering, or shrines. We shall see in the next two chapters that this somewhat surreal polyvalency is essential to understanding Greco-Roman myths about the origins of Doric, Ionic, and Corinthian.

3

Images of Temple Founders

The Shrine of Aphrodite at Paphos

We have been reconstructing a Hellenistic myth about the origins of the orders. That myth, of course, does not necessarily teach us what prompted Bronze Age Greeks to build the first temples: we do not really know, on the basis of the evidence given, that the real founders of the orders conceived of their temples as groves of sacred trees and that they decorated them with σπλάγχνα. We only know that certain Greco-Roman writers used architectural terms suggesting that *they* thought about temple architecture this way. By Hellenistic times, moreover, classical architectural ornament had achieved the full degree of abstraction by which we know it; the names of the ornaments and moldings might have suggested sacrificial origins, but their forms did not. There was, however, one ancient temple, famous throughout the Mediterranean, that was clearly constructed from sacrificial components.

I have in mind the Temple of Aphrodite at Paphos on the island of Cyprus. Paphos was one of the oldest, richest, and most famous of all ancient Greek holy places. The original temple was erected in c. 1200 B.C., and at its height the complex consisted of colonnades and halls, colored mosaic pavements, and gardens surrounded by a grove of sacred trees.[1] The focus was a holy stone, or baetyl, which still exists (figure 22). It is a black meteorite worshiped as the goddess's aniconic image fallen from heaven. We recall the story: Saturn quarreled with his father Uranus, cut off the paternal penis, and flung it into the sea off Paphos. When it hit the foam, it turned into Aphrodite.[2] Hence the baetyl images both Uranus's member and the goddess of love. It is thought that the shrine at Paphos was fronted by a pool, which would symbolize this

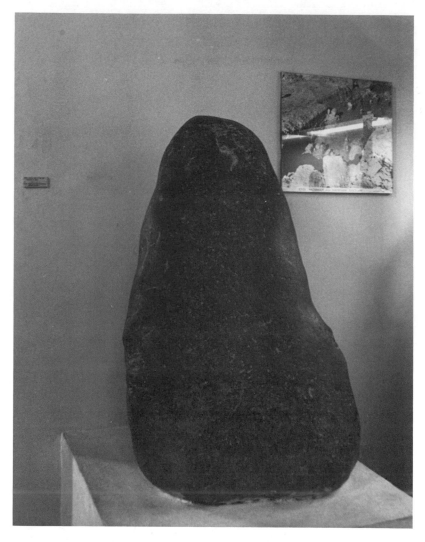

22
Baetyl or meteorite from
the shrine of Aphrodite,
Paphos. Cyprus Museum,
Nicosia.

watery transformation.[3] The goddess's votaries, meanwhile, carried bowls of salt in their processions to represent the sea-foam that troped Aphrodite's name, ἄφρος. Moreover, the goddess was known locally as Paphia, which similarly tropes παφλάζω, bubble up, foam. The votaries also carried phalloi, representing the thing the salt or foam had transformed.[4]

The shrine containing the baetyl was apparently quite small. Roman coins dating from the reign of Augustus through that of Philippus Arabs, 244–249 A.D., with an interregnum during the second century, present a remarkably consistent image of the shrine (figures 23–25). The facade is clearly of a preclassical type, and it is set in a semicircular temenos surrounded by a fence or balustrade.[5] (The pattern is not unique, however, as a model shrine from Vounous, also on Cyprus, portrays a similar temple from c. 2000 B.C.[6]) The similarity of these depictions, which of course may not accurately reflect the original temple, suggests that the building's image had value as a souvenir and perhaps talisman — that the design was a sort of logo.

The temenos, in most coins, is occupied by a bird and what I take to be eggs. The bird is probably a dove, sacred both to Aphrodite and to Astarte, Aphrodite's opposite number from the Near East, who was born when a dove hatched her from an egg and who was also worshiped on Cyprus.[7] Aphrodite came to be associated with doves as well, and her votaries, especially, were so identified.[8] Temples kept flocks of these and other birds, while eggs and bird claws, as we saw, decorated liturgical objects.[9] At Paphos two more doves flank the central pair of towers, which creates a roughly triangular, that is, tympanum-like, silhouette on the upper part of the main pavilion. (We recall that Pindar had claimed that the first temple tympanum was surmounted by eagles[10] and that in Greek the raking cornice of the tympanum was generally called the ἀετός). Votive statues from Cypriote shrines of Aphrodite also carry doves, presumably as offerings to the goddess.[11]

The central pair of columns have horned capitals.[12] We saw in the last chapter that Cypriote priests wore horned headgear. The arrangement also strongly resembles horned shrines found in

23
Large bronze coin of
Septimus Severus,
depicting the shrine at
Paphos. From Félix
Lajard, *Recherches sur le
culte de Vénus,* Paris, 1849.

24
Large bronze coin of
Caracalla, depicting the
shrine at Paphos. From
Félix Lajard, *Recherches sur
le culte de Vénus,* Paris,
1849.

25
The shrine of Aphrodite.
From T. L. Donaldson,
Architectura numismatica,
London, 1859.

26
Vase with idol, Early
Bronze Age (2000–1900
B.C.). Cyprus Museum,
Nicosia.

Bronze Age Cypriote tombs (figure 26). These horns undoubtedly reflect the sacrificial slaughter of animals, although Herodotus tells us that blood was not allowed to flow on the altar of Paphos (7.195.2). But the horns at Paphos had at least a double meaning. Lucian calls the similar columns set before the temple of the Dea Syria in Hieropolis phalloi, and phalloi were so important in Paphiote worship that these columns must also portray the organs.[13] Not only were human-scale phalloi carried in processions (and throughout Greece, not just at Paphos), but colossal ones were erected throughout the Greek-speaking world.[14]

If the columns were phalloi, they were only gigantic surrogates for the true phallus that was the baetyl itself. But the Roman coins transform even the baetyl into architectural forms such as the urn or the obelisk (figures 23, 24). In his *Thesaurus*, A. F. Gori prints one with the head and torso of a woman, which specifically expresses the transformation of Uranus's member.[15] Whatever form the baetyl takes in these images, they are all what might be called architectural embodiments of the goddess. Aphrodite Paphia, in short, is the central column or stele in a group of other columns.[16] And while the central columns are all primitive embodiments, those of the flanking pavilions seem to have become orthodox Ionic by the time the Roman coins were struck.[17] This, by the way, would trope the word for dove, ἰωνάς.

In short, Aphrodite's shrine was not merely garnished with but was built up from objects used by worshipers in her cult. And in addition to the horned columns, the baetyl, the doves, the eggs, and the water, there was, hanging between the main columns, a crescent or garland and just above that a star. Both these shapes are associated, again, with Aphrodite's sister-goddess on Cyprus, Astarte.[18] But the sacrifices enacted at Paphos were a far cry from those we have been discussing. The Cypriote town was a center for the ἱερὸς γάμος, sacred prostitution.[19] The prostitutes were considered priestesses and called ἱερόδουλοι, temple servants. In religion their act was a union between the client (worshiper) and Aphrodite. Just as a slaughtered animal became the vessel of a god, so Aphrodite's prostitute could incarnate the goddess.[20] The horns of the shrine at Paphos, then, seem to represent a traditional sacrificial element in the temple's architecture, preserved after the prohibition of blood sacrifice. But the columns for which those horns form capitals, and the doves and eggs, clearly represent the cult of sacred marriage.

The Dorians' First Shrines

Like so many Greek temples, the Paphiote shrine was the image and home of the founder of a cult. Vitruvius describes the first Doric and Ionic temples similarly. Furthermore, these temples are also linked to marriage, but the marriages take place against the background of war and blood sacrifice.

Vitruvius says the Doric order was invented by Dorus, son of Hellen and the nymph Phthia.[21] Dorus represented a race of conquerors. As the father of the Dorian peoples, he ruled one of four basic subdivisions of the Greek population, the others being the Aeolians, the Ionians, and the Achaeans. All three latter races were said to have been at times subject to Dorus's followers (Apollodorus, *The Library*, 1.7.3). His method of conquest seems to have been to wander from region to region with his band of soldiers, killing off or driving out the indigenous populations. He reigned temporarily as Lord of the Peloponnese, which was called after him at that period (Herodotus, 1.56). But later he wandered to northern Greece, where he was slain (Apollodorus, *The Library*, 1.7.4, 1.7.6).

The words "Dorus" and "Dorian" contain more than the flavor of racial conquest. They are tropes of violence. δορά means flayed skin; δορατίζωμαι means fighting with spears, from δόρυ, spear or scepter. There are many similar compounds of δόρυ, as well as such homonyms as δορίαλλος, female genitals, which is particularly close to δοριάλωτος, meaning captive of the spear, one who is taken in war. δορυφορέω and its derivatives also refer to guards and imprisonment. Δορυκλείοι, which means those of Dorian glory, was the epithet of Dorian warriors (Pausanias, 1.1.40). So the picture is one of death by the spear, accompanied by sexual menace.

These tropes well suit ancient Greek warfare. It was common practice for a victorious army to slaughter all enemy males and children and make concubines of the women (*Iliad*, 9.591ff., 24.732ff.; *Odyssey*, 8.523ff.).[22] Here is Priam describing war to Hector: "the massacre of my sons, my daughters mauled, their bedrooms pillaged, their babies dashed on the ground by the brutal enemy, and my sons' wives hauled away by foul Achaean hands."[23] Indeed, as R. B. Onians points out, the whole of the *Iliad* is built up of quarrels based on these practices.[24]

I have mentioned the trophies that were erected on the spot where a victorious soldier put his enemy to death. Battle itself was often perceived, in art and literature, as arrays of powerful male figures standing like close-set columns. Thus Tyrtaios:

So let [each man] fight toe to toe, pressing shield against shield,
    crest against crest, helm against helm,
and chest against chest, drawing near his man,
    gripping the hilt of his sword or the length of his spear . . .

And when in the *Iliad* (2.40) Agamemnon dreams of taking Troy in a day, he sees his Greeks defeating the Trojans in one-on-one encounters. The notion of men (and women) in close-set array pervaded other activities. On a Late Geometric I amphora in Athens (figure 27), we see mourners bearing garlands that make rectangular niches for their upright bodies and raised arms. They stand like warriors—or colonnades. Indeed one type of highly columnar statue, the colossus, *is* a column, for the words are related: "colossus" originally meant column-like (figure 28).[25] Put differently, as "colossus" and "column" are tropes, so are the things those words stand for.

Vitruvius describes the first Doric temple in this spirit. It was built by Dorus himself, in Argos, and dedicated to Juno. (And there is in fact a very ancient shrine to Juno, i.e., Hera, there—one of the earliest buildings to have standard Greek temple form.[26]) Later on, Vitruvius adds, other Doric temples were constructed throughout the cities of Achaea (the northern edge of the Peloponnese):

27
Late Geometric I amphora
by the Dipylon Master
(850–750 B.C.). National
Muscum, Athens. (Photo:
Deutsche Archäologische
Institut, Athens)

28
The "Auxerre Goddess,"
probably Cretan, c. 630
B.C. Musée du Louvre,
Paris. (Photo: Art
Resource)

Afterward the Athenians, in accordance with the responses of Apollo, and by the general consent of all Greece, founded thirteen colonies in Asia at one time. They appointed chiefs in the several colonies, and gave the supreme authority to Ion, the son of Xuthus and Creusa (whom Apollo, in his responses at Delphi, had declared to be his son). He led the colonies into Asia and seized the territory of Caria. In and around that region he established the large cities of Ephesus, Miletus, Myus [etc.]. These cities drove out the Carians and Leleges and renamed the area Ionia from their leader Ion and, establishing there sanctuaries of the immortal gods, they began to build temples in them. First, to Pan-Ionian Apollo[27] they established a temple based on those they had known in Achaea. Then they called it Doric because they had first seen it built in in the Dorian cities. When they wished to place the columns in that temple, not having their proportions, and seeking by what method they could make them fit to bear weight, and in their appearance to have an approved grace, they measured a man's footstep and applied it to his height. Finding that the foot was the sixth part of the height in a man, they applied this proportion to the column. . . . So the Doric column began to furnish the proportion of a man's body, its strength and grace (4.1.5, 4.1.6).

Vitruvius's story accords with the facts at least to the extent that Apollo (and Artemis) were worshiped in Ionia as colonization divinities.[29] And here again one supposes that the wartime customs of δορίαλλος and δοριάλωτος were followed, no doubt accompanied by sacrifices to these divinities. Indeed, Vitruvius emphasizes the warfare between the Dorians and the native tribes, some of whom "devastated the Greeks cruelly" (2.8.12). On the occasions when the Greeks were victorious, however, these indigenes, in the normal fashion, would have provided the invaders with women (Herodotus, 1.146).

The Doric order was now reconstituted by Ion so as to memorialize these events. I infer from Vitruvius's language that the use of male proportions in the columns was a novelty, that is, the earlier temples of the Peloponnese did not have such proportions. Vitruvius also implies that this second, Ionian Doric became definitive. And, as a matter of historic fact, the earliest Doric temples were indeed far from the later norm (though that norm apparently did not first develop in Ionia).[30] Vitruvius says the Doric order is named and shaped after the Dorian man. But that man, of course, is named after Dorus, who in any case built the first Doric temple, in mainland Greece. This gives the order the quality of an ancestor-image. And indeed Clement of Alexandria claims that *all* temples are basically monuments to ancestors and are the tombs of men and women who have been deified and are now worshiped (*Protrepticon*, 3.39, 4.49).

As Vitruvius further implies, the chief god and goddess of the Ionian Greeks were the brother and sister Artemis and Apollo. This is logical since, as Vitruvius notes, Ion was Apollo's son.[31] Caria was filled with shrines to Apollo, and in Vitruvius's account the newly reinvented Doric columns adorned a temple to him. Since these columns are twice likened to naked men (4.1.6, 4.1.7) and since, as we know from innumerable vase paintings, Greeks by artistic convention (though not in reality) fought in the nude (and seemingly mourned so, see figure 27), we may take it that the reconstituted Doric columns portrayed or recalled these Dorian invaders. Just as the architecturalized baetyl at Paphos represented the temple's founder, here in Ionia architecturalized images of founders were formed into temples.

The Doric column as Vitriuvius here describes it, aside from its "nudity," has only a proportional relationship to the Dorian man. But one further, less-noticed way in which Vitruvius humanizes the column is by using the word *entasis* (3.3.13). This means tension, straining, exertion and can refer to the human body.[32] Vitruvius uses it to describe the slight outward curvature in the silhouette of the Doric shaft. This notion, of architectural supports seen as straining human figures, will come into play in my discussions of the caryatid and Persian porticoes. But already, in Vitruvius's myth, one can imagine as columns the military arrays of abstract figures bearing wreaths or other gifts as sacrifices to the dead, their arms raised as if to support the forms above them, which, among the meanders, zigzags, and other decorations of vases that are so often architectural, seem like the fascias of an entablature (figure 27). A similar columnar quality inhabits any number of statues (figure 28).

Whatever the historic reality of such a thing as the Dorian race, any number of Doric temples were erected by Greek colonist-invaders. I will mention only one of the best known and most impressive, the so-called Basilica (a temple to Hera) at Paestum. Paestum was founded at the end of the seventh century B.C. by Achaean Greek colonists from Sybaris who drove out the local Lucanian peoples. In the middle of the sixth century they erected the oldest of the three great Doric temples that stand by the shore. Today, perhaps more than when they were built, these columns do indeed resemble files of gigantic warriors marching ashore, armed and menacing, bearing aloft their weapons and supplies (figure 29).[33]

Doric temples, from the earliest times through the Parthenon and beyond, are very often ornamented with sculpture, usually on the tympana, consisting of images of battle, murder, and sacrifice. The battles depicted in the corners of the Temple of Artemis at Corfu are among the best-known examples.[34] Of the seventy-three tympana dating from 600 to 325 B.C. that Lapalus catalogued in *Le Fronton sculpté en Grèce*, more than half depict mortal struggles.[35] From Aegina, with its combats before the walls of Troy, through Athens, with its innumerable sculptured wars and deaths (e.g., the Temple of Athena Nike, the Hephaisteion, the Parthenon), to the Gigantomachy on the frieze at Sounion, to the battle of centaurs on the east gable of the Temple of Asklepios at Epidauros, the sculptures reenact the struggle embodied in the first tympanum, which Pindar defined as a restrainer of violent horses.

Ion and the Ionians

Violent scenes are also found on Ionic temples, though the Ionic order has traditionally been connected with women and been called graceful and pretty in comparison to the Doric. But in Vitruvius's myth, the women of the Ionic order, though captives, are far from passive.

Afterward also seeking to plan a temple of Diana in a new kind of style, they [the Dorians] changed [the Doric column] to a feminine

29
Paestum. Temples of Hera
and Poseidon. (Photo: Art
Resource)

slenderness using the same measurement by feet. And first they made the diameter of the column the eighth part of it, that it might have more beauty. Under the base they placed a convex molding in the manner of a sandal [here we recall that βάσις means foot and dance measure]; at the capital they put volutes, like graceful curling hair hanging over right and left. And, arranging cymatia and festoons in a coiffure, they ornamented the face. Then they let fluting fall across the body like the folds of matronly robes (4.1.7; see figure 10).

I shall assume that this second order was also Ion's creation, since this part of the account directly follows the section in which Ion is the group's leader.

Though it portrays a woman, Ion has named this second order after himself. He was not without feminine qualities, as the tropes of his name make clear. ἴον is a violet or gilliflower, ἰονθάς means thick, curling hair, and ἴονθος is a lock of hair. Ἰόνιος means named for Io, Zeus's beautiful companion. (And let us recall, too, that Io was horned). ἰωντᾶς, dove, is even closer to the Greek for Ion, Ἰών. (We saw the Ionic columns at dove-haunted Paphos.) ἰωνικός, meanwhile, in addition to meaning Ionic or Ionian, means effeminate and refers as well to a soft, elegant poetic meter.

And tropes are part of Ion's identity. In Euripides, Hermes names him (*Ion*, 80). It is later revealed that Ion's mother, Creusa, daughter of Erechtheus, king of Athens, had slept with Apollo (she calls it a sacred marriage; 946, 1285), though the servant uses the name Ion as a trope, saying that Creusa simply *came upon* the child, Ἴων, ἰόντι δήθεν ὅτι συνήντετο (831; ἴων means, or can mean, coming upon). I should perhaps add that Creusa was herself a battle spoil. She was given to Xuthus as the trophy of his spear, δορὸς λαβὼν γέρας (298). At the end of Euripides's play, that "doric" gift results in a prediction by Athena that Ion's offspring will people Ionia, while his brother Dorus will beget the Doric race (1586ff.).

But we must not forget that the names Ion and Ionia overlie the earlier Carian, which persisted despite the competition. Κὰρ is Carian in Greek, and it also means mercenary soldier. The word tropes κάρα or κάρη, which means variously hair, face, and head.

Hair is associated not only with women but also with military exploits. Homer is always calling soldiers "long-haired Achaians" (*Iliad*, 2.51, for example). In Apollodorus, when Medusa was decapitated, she was ἐκαρατομήθη, de-*kara*ed. But the most important trope is κέρας, horn, which brings into the Carian/Ionic order all the associations of that word. In short, a Carian column is one that tropes head, face, hair, and horns.

The feminine and military elements combine again in Ion's worship of Artemis. She had many shrines and temples in Caria, and of course the most famous of all her temples stood at neighboring Ephesus.[36] Vitruvius says this was the first Ionic temple ever dedicated to her (7, Pref. 16), which accords to some extent with historic fact.[37] We have seen Artemis as a hunting goddess and as the patroness of the cruel rites of Patras, but she was also a military goddess. It was she to whom the Greeks prayed in their victories over the Persians (Aristophanes, *Lysistrata*, 1248ff.). And she could be bloodthirsty; in early times she demanded human sacrifices.[38] It is not surprising, then, that her name has tropes, even etymologies, of violence. Liddell and Scott say the name Artemis is probably derived from ἄρταμος, murderer, butcher. In Doric the goddess's name is in fact spelled "Artamis," and ἀρταμέω means to cut into pieces, and ἀρτάω to bind or hang. So the tropes of the Ionic order, though female and ornamental, are as bloody as those of the Doric, if not more so.

The Death of a Corinthian κόρη

The last of Vitruvius's myths about the origins of the orders deals with what might be called the absence of marriage. It tells how the Corinthian capital was born.[39] This too takes place in an atmosphere of death and sacrifice, though these are not violent. Vitruvius relates that one day Callimachus, an architect, spotted the tomb of a young Corinthian woman who had died just before her marriage. Her nurse had decorated the tomb with a basket containing her prized collection of goblets and had laid a tile on top to keep them in place. An acanthus plant had grown up from the base of the basket, and its tendrils were curled back by the tile. Callimachus transformed the little tableau into the Corinthian capital (figure 12). Some details were original (4.1.9), but others were borrowed from the Doric and Ionic orders (4.1.1).[40]

Vitruvius's story belongs to the tradition in which trees and plants serve as tombs. For instance, a cherry tree was planted as a tomb on Geryon's grave after Hercules had slain him, and a pomegranate on that of Menoicus.[41] That tradition, in turn, is linked not only to the sacred tree but also to the idea that the dead metamorphose into plants, as Adonis became an anemone and Daphne became a laurel tree. In Ovid Venus consecrates the anemone that Adonis had become and calls it a "monument" (*Metamorphoses*, 10.725).

Like the Doric and Ionic orders, therefore, the Corinthian memorializes, but it marks a premature death rather than the marriage of invaders to their female captives. And, more than Doric and Ionic, Corinthian has the sense of a specific sacrifice. The nurse in Vitruvius's tale is the canephoros or basket carrier of tomb sacrifice;[42] and the goblets in the basket she bears not only reflect the custom of filling tombs with the favorite objects of the dead person, but also recall the practice of pouring libations of wine over the burnt bones of the newly dead.[43] Vitruvius has probably asked us to picture a columnar tomb such as was common in the Greek world from the third century B.C. onward. These sometimes have carved acanthus plants round the base and baskets or urns on top (figure 30). It is common for carved acanthus leaves to grow up from the base of a column shaft, or even, in Hellenistic times, from the base of each drum.

Callimachus is a historic figure, mentioned both by Pliny and Pausanias.[44] He built monuments in Corinth and was a famous bronze-caster, which may be why some believe that originally "Corinthian capital" meant a capital made of bronze rather than stone.[45] One of his masterpieces in Athens was the lamp in the temple of Athena Polias that burned before the image. Callimachus was known by the epithet κατάτεχνος, the artificial. Pausanias renders this as κατατηξίτεχνος, refiner of art, which nicely relates

30
Funeral urn, fourth
century B.C. National
Museum, Athens.

to the tropes of his name. "Callimachus" suggests κάλλος, beautiful, and all its many compounds and variants. So Callimachus has something to do with beauty; and καλλιμάχομαι would mean struggle with (or for) beauty, or even to dispute about, or compete in, beauty. Similarly, a καλλίμαχη would be a battle of beauty, or conceivably a beautiful battle. So, albeit in attenuated form, the invention of the Corinthian order partakes of the mood of battle that informs the Doric and Ionic.

To us the word "Corinthian" simply means something or someone associated with Corinth. It had this meaning in Greek, of course, but there were other associations. First of all, especially in Vitruvius's context, it can be seen as a compound of κόρη, young girl. Κόρη, the proper name, is meanwhile an epithet for Persephone, Pluto's consort in the Underworld, queen of the shades of the departed, akin to Scotia, and worshiped each spring as the force that drives up from earth the flowers and vegetables of the new season. She is especially a grain goddess, and here one thinks of the related word κόρηθρον, broom plant, and all *its* relatives. In any event, a *buried* Cor-inthian maiden would have to bring Kore to mind.

But the maidens, the κόραι, of Corinth were above all famous because the city was a second Paphos. The verb Κορινθιάζομαι, I Corinthize, so to speak, means to have sex with a prostitute. And when Plato says the man who wants to keep fit should not have a mistress, he uses the word κόρη Κορινθή, Corinthian girl (*Republic*, 404d). In Corinth the most famous site for sacred marriage was the temple of Aphrodite Melainis at Kraneion. Inscriptions document the existence of over a thousand prostitutes in service here at the time of the Persian Wars.[46] It could even be that in lost versions of the tale Vitruvius tells the Corinthian girl actually *was* a sacred prostitute—hence the emphasis on the fact that she had amassed possessions (a dowry) but was not yet married. "Acanthus," on the other hand, while of course it means the plant, has many tropes emphasizing that plant's prickliness. ἄκανθα, as opposed to ἄκανθος, the bear's-foot, means thorn or prickle in general. Variants mean spine or backbone, as of a fish or mammal, or even a hedgehog.[47] All this would link the Corinthian capital to the Doric with its thorn-painted echinus. And indeed both Corinthian and Ionic capitals can have echini, usually decorated with egg-and-claw moldings (figure 14). The girl's collection of cups, her dowry or treasure, is sealed within this thorny bush. In fact the basket is more than sealed off; in the vast majority of Corinthian capitals (figure 12), it is completely hidden by the leafy growth.[48] So the latest of the three capitals, curiously, does the most to return us to the idea of the sacred tree and also to the atmosphere of sacred marriage that pervaded Paphos.

That return has a kind of finality. As noted, the Corinthian order is comprised of details from Doric and Ionic. It is therefore in a sense the daughter of the original male and female orders. But the girl's death before marriage prevents new offspring; there will be no new types of column. With this final invention the pattern of Vitruvius's three Greek tales about the intervention of the orders is complete.[49]

4

The Caryatid and Persian Porticoes

The Women of Caryae

Vitruvius tells two historical tales that complement the myths we have just reviewed. The first is the story of the Caryatids (1.1.5). He says that the architectural supports known by this name (figure 31) were invented during the Persian Wars, in the late fifth century B.C. During these invasions some smaller Greek states, among them the town of Caryae in northern Laconia, conspired with the enemy.[1] After the invaders were defeated and driven away, all Greece turned against the traitorous town. In Caryae the result was a variation of the δορίαλλος, δοριάλωτος scenario.

[It] was captured and all the menfolk killed. The married women were led off in captivity, and they were not allowed to remove the stoles and ornament that showed them to be married women. They were led through the city not in the manner of a triumphal procession held on a single occasion but rather were displayed before the city as permanent examples sustaining a weight of punishment for their heavy sins. Thus the architects of that time designed for public buildings figures of matrons placed to carry burdens; in order that the punishment of the sin of the Caryaean women might be known to posterity and historically recorded.

In other words, as I read the passage, instead of being made into concubines, the matrons were set into a multiple pillory that made them look like piers or columns. Pierre Ducrey speculates that ἀποτυμπανισμός, being set under a tympanum, involved being tied to pillars[2] (which recalls Pindar's reading of the tympanum as a subduer of violence), but the word itself has to mean any pillars that support a tympanum. This in turn suggests the Roman phrase *sub corona*, being set under the crown or cornice, that is, in a real or metaphorical pillory. Pillorying, and its near ally crucifixion,

31
Athens, The Erechtheum,
Porch of the Maidens,
begun 421 B.C. (Photo: Art
Resource)

were considered particularly appropriate punishments for traitors.[3] In any event, the classical literature contains many descriptions of columns with prisoners bound to them (Sophocles, *Ajax*,
107, 239).

"Caryatid," meanwhile, means simply inhabitant (or child) of
Caryae. The homonym καρύα is a nut tree, usually walnut, while
χάρια, which has almost the same sound,[4] is given by Hesychius,
the ancient lexical authority, as variously meaning hill, mound,
blood clot, or altar. The word, in short, contains the tropes of a
shrine where blood sacrifices take place.

But the central group of words that concern us relates to the
town Vitruvius mentions, the north Spartan mountain community
of Καρύαι. Located there was a famous temple of Artemis, whose
priestesses were called καρυάτιδες. Every year the town's youth
performed a dance called the caryatis around an outdoor statue of
the goddess.[5] Καρυᾶτις was also, naturally enough, an epithet for
Artemis herself (Pausanias, 3.10.7, 3.10.8).

There are other associations as well. The adjective κήρ, meaning
an inhabitant of the nearly eponymous Caria, applied to slaves
generally.[6] Κήρ, on the other hand, with a capital, is the goddess of
death (*Odyssey*, 11.171). And κήρ means heart, especially in the
sense of the bodily organ with its complex network of veins and
arteries. The κήρ of a sacrificed animal was displayed on a tree,
altar, or obelisk. κήρ was also often fused with κήρ into a force for
evil, a taboo.[7] Nor can one ignore the trope between *Cor*inthan and
*Car*yatid, which would apply many of the above associations to Callimachus's order. Above all, we note that κήρ means coiled horn.
Further, the Asian Carians, like the Spartan ones in Vitruvius's
story, were notorious for their treachery.[8] Sometimes they were also
identified with slaves, and with the κήρες, goddesses of death, or
souls of the dead.[9]

There was a young woman named Carya as well. She was the
daughter of King Dion of Laconia, and, it was said, had refused
the love of Dionysus. He punished her by turning her into a καρύα
or walnut tree.[10] So Carya is a woman turned into a sacred tree,
just as Callimachus's nameless Corinthian maiden becomes a sa-

cred bush. Artemis's favorite virtue, chastity, is paramount here. It was Carya's chastity, her refusal to be suborned by a god, that led the Caryaeans to honor Artemis.[11] And on another occasion Aristomenes, leading the revolt of the Messenians against their Spartan occupiers, seized the most aristocratic Caryatids as they were dancing and placed them under guard. The guards tried to rape the girls. Just in time Aristomenes intervened, and while he punished the guards, he also demanded ransom for the girls' return. This was paid, and the Caryatids were restored unharmed to their towns.[12]

The caryatis dance leads us to the most famous function of architectural caryatids. The women raised their arms during the dance, just as women at sacrifices raised theirs when the god came into their presence. A fragment from the playwright Lyncaeus shows that the raised arms of caryatis dancers could also be interpreted as supporting weight. A character, Eucrates, scoffs at a group of people partying in a room whose ceiling is about to collapse. He says to them, "You eat with your right hands but with your left you have to hold up the ceiling like the caryatids" (Lyncaeus, *Frag.*, 6.241d). It is interesting that these people—and Lyncaeus does not exclude the possibility that some are males—are not being punished but are in the position of forced support.

A caryatid porch, finally, has the associations we have already seen in Doric and Ionic—associations with Caria, with Artemis, with militant female chastity, and with women captives. For I am assuming that Vitruvius's errant Caryaean women had submitted to the Persians in accordance with the custom of the δοριάλωτος. If so, their punishment not only fitted, but troped, their crime: as concubines, they danced the chastity dance in architectural perpetuity.

Vitruvius's caryatids are in several respects negative versions of those of the Erechtheum (figure 31). And the latter, in turn, bring up the whole question of Greek and Roman *Stützfiguren* or statue-columns. Before the Erechtheum, Greek statue-columns were usually in pairs, flanking entrances. The Erechtheum figures, being six in number, are probably unusual for their period.[13] They are also like the troop of figures envisaged in Vitruvius's tale. The Athenian temple, moreover, was built to replace one destroyed by the Persian invaders of Athens in 480 B.C. so it shares its occasion, at least in Vitruvius's version of the story, with the portico at Caryae.[14]

And yet the caryatids of the Erechtheum are clearly not punished prisoners, nor do they raise their arms. Artemis does not appear to have a connection with this temple, and the women are not matrons but girls, παρθένοι. Indeed, the earliest written document for the statues calls them κόραι, maidens,[15] not caryatids. (One notes however that "Caryae" and "korai" are tropes.)

The Erechtheum was constructed over the tomb of one of Athens's early mythical kings, Erechtheus. In a way such a building, as a House of Erechtheus,[16] was Athena's primary dwelling in Athens (*Odyssey*, 7.81). During Erechtheus's reign, Eumolpos, son of Poseidon, came with an army of Thracians to conquer the city. Before the battle Apollo told Erechtheus that to assure a victory he would have to sacrifice one of his daughters, of whom (according to an ancient compendium of Euripides fragments[17]) he had six. In several versions of the story, the other daughters are also sacrificed, or else they commit suicide in order to be with their sister.[18] During the battle, Erechtheus killed Eumolpos; this was accepted by Poseidon as an atoning sacrifice.[19] Afterward, Erechtheus's heroic παρθένοι were honored and placed in the heavens among the Hyades or Hyacinthides,[20] and they received divine honors and sacrifices on the occasion of every subsequent Athenian military expedition.[21] And ever afterward, too, the cults of the Athenian acropolis were in the hands of a family, the Etioboutadai, that claimed descent from Erechtheus.[22]

According to Euripides (*Ion*, 260), Erechtheus had another daughter, Creusa, who did not die with her sisters because she was still an infant at the time of the battle. We have already seen that Creusa became the mother of Ion, who went on to found the Doric and Ionic orders. Ionic, naturally, was used on the Erechtheum. Euripides also tells us of events leading to the construction of the Erechtheum. In *Erechtheus*, whose ending has recently come to light, Athena addresses the dead king's wife, Praxithea: "For your husband I command a shrine to be constructed in the middle of the city; he will be known for him who killed him, under the name of 'sacred Poseidon' [i.e., temple of Poseidon]; but among the citizens, when the sacrificial cattle are slaughtered, he shall be called 'Erechtheus.'"[23] And the Erechtheum is indeed a temple to Poseidon.[24] Moreover I suggest that the "caryatid porch" of the Erechtheum, with its six young women supporting an Ionic entablature, is a monument to these events. It would also be a *contre-coup* to Vitruvius's caryatid portico at Caryae, making the two porticoes, respectively, examples of noble and punitive female sacrifice.[25]

The Persian Warriors

Vitruvius's second myth also contains the themes of sacrifice and Greek victories over Persians. Immediately after his tale of the Caryaean women, he adds that when, in this same invasion, Spartan troops under a general named Pausanias (not the writer) conquered an infinitely larger Persian force, they built a portico "as a trophy of victory to their descendants."

There they placed statues of their captives in barbaric dress—punishing their pride with deserved insults—to support the roof, that their enemies might quake, fearing the workings of such bravery, and that their fellow citizens, looking upon a pattern of manhood, might by such glory be roused and prepared for the defense of freedom. Therefrom many have set up Persian statues to support architraves and their ornaments (1.1.6).

We know that there was indeed a Persian portico at Sparta (Pausanias, 3.11.3) which had, addorsed to its columns, white marble statues of Persian prisoners. In Vitruvius's version the story is a retelling of the Caryaean tale with the substitution of Persian men for Greek women. So the "Persids" are mates, of sorts, for the Caryatids.[26] But they are battlefield trophies too, images of defeated foes.[27] Vitruvius in fact says the Spartans *pro tropaeo constituerunt* their portico, erected it *as* a trophy. Hugh Plommer publishes a

relief in the Museo Nazionale, Naples, of a pair of caryatids holding aloft a roof (using one arm each, like Eucrates's friends) while
a prisoner sits before a trophy. The inscription reads τῆι Ἑλλάδι
τὸ τρόπαιον ἐστάθη, "[Someone] set up the trophy to Greece." It
has been suspected that the inscription is forged, and the piece
itself is probably Hadrianic. But even so, Plommer thinks it may be
based on a fourth-century B.C. Greek work.[28] And the sculpture
clearly associated prisoners of war and architectural caryatids.
Whatever the case with the Naples piece, in Vitruvius the Persian
portico is presented as an intermediary between the temple and
secular architecture.

The human content of the Doric, Ionic, and Corinthian orders
is both patent and implicit. But in Vitruvius the more sculptural
cousins of the three basic orders are fully anthropo- and gyneco-
morphic. The elements of ancestral strife and the founding of
buildings as ways of mediating or resolving that strife are also present. Indeed, the stories of the caryatid and Persian porticoes give
to architecture a distinctly punitive aspect. They reinforce its role
as the exhibitor of justice accomplished.

5

Francesco di Giorgio, Michelangelo, and Raphael

Vitruvius's teachings about the origin of the orders and the meaning of ornament had a dense but checkered destiny in the Renaissance. There is a great deal to the subject. Here I shall only point to a few major instances that extend, rather than simply repeat, the foregoing ideas.

First of all we find little trace of the Greek Vitruvius in the earlier part of the quattrocento. Until at least the 1480s there were almost no reliable Vitruvius manuscripts and many quite unreliable ones. In such manuscripts, Greek words were manhandled or else omitted entirely, even when the result was nonsense.[1] So it is not surprising that the earliest modern writers of architectural treatises, Alberti and Filarete, pay little attention to Vitruvius's Greek terms. But it is surprising that they also leave out the Greek myths and legends of which Vitruvius makes so much. Alberti, it is true, has a few phrases on Callimachus and the invention of the Corinthian order; but he has little or nothing on Dorus, Ion, and even the names for moldings.

Filarete is less easily dismissed. He illustrates, but does not comment on, columns consisting of male figures, which unlike traditional *Stützfiguren* do indeed seem to struggle with their burden (figure 32), straining their bodies and using their arms to relieve the weight on their heads, "almost crushed by the superincumbent weight" (Vitruvius, 1.1.5, 1.1.6). Alternatively, however, Filarete's columns could be seen as representing the Doric order, for Vitruvius twice says that Doric represents the nude male body (4.1.6, 4.1.7; yet the entablatures in Filarete's drawing are not Doric). A closer match would be the male support-figures on the Olympaeum at Agrigento (figure 33), fragments of which existed at the

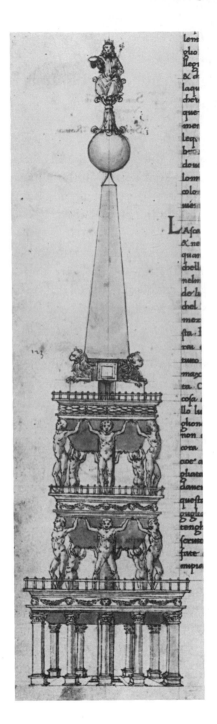

32
Filarete, Fountain. From
the Magliabecchiano
Codex, Biblioteca
Nazionale, Florence, folio
102v.

33
Agrigento, Olympaeum,
begun c. 500 B.C. From
R. Koldewey and O. Puch-
stein, *Die griechischen Tempel
in Unteritalien und Sizilien,*
1899.

site, and which were in any case described in these poses by
Pausanias.[2]

There was one architectural writer of the early Renaissance, of
course, whose love of things Greek matched Vitruvius's. That was
Francesco Colonna, reputed author of the *Hypnerotomachia Poli-
phili.* But Colonna, though he strews his prose with Greek words
and attributes the quattrocento-style designs in his book to Greek
architects such as Lychas of Libya, pays as little attention to the
questions addressed by this book as do Alberti and Filarete.

Francesco di Giorgio

Francesco di Giorgio is a different matter. He wrote a book in the
1480s apparently based on a corrupt pastiche of Vitruvius's text
and then revised it in successive versions into the 1490s, when he
had more reliable texts in hand. Each version of Francesco's book
is divided into separate treatises.[3] Like Alberti and Filarete, Francesco omits the legends of the Caryaean women and the Persian
captives. But the Doric, Ionic, and Corinthian stories are retold, as
far as I know, for the first time in modern literature. Sometimes
these are delightfully misread. Thus when the Dorians go to Asia
they found not thirteen *Ionian colonies* but thirteen *Ionic columns*.[4]

That certainly fits in with the construction I have put on Vitruvius's stories. And Francesco presents the origin of the Corinthian capital as follows:

A young woman citizen of Corinth, still unmarried, died of an illness. Whence her tomb. The girl's nurse took the embalmed [body], in a tapered basket full of earth, to a grove the girl had enjoyed during her lifetime, carried it to the burial place, and placed it on top. And, so that the body would the longer remain undisturbed, she covered the basket with a tile. By chance the basket was set on the root of an acanthus plant in such a way that, the root being pressed down by the weight, the leaves in the center of the bush, in accordance with their width and the basket's weight, sprang up around the corners [of the basket] and were tightly curled back into volutes.[5]

So Vitruvius's basket of goblets, placed on the girl's tomb, is turned into a basket-sarcophagus for the girl herself.

Francesco's illustration, curiously enough, shows both the outer basket and the young woman's body within it, arms crossed at her waist (figure 34). In another sketch on the same page he repeats this idea, but now the girl within is shown separately from the outer basket and the basket itself is a column, labeled *colonna stolata,* that is, wrapped in a stole braided around the shaft (figure 35). (We recall that Vitruvius's caryatids wore stoles.) The girl, furthermore, is bound like a prisoner. Conceivably this too may have something to do with Vitruvius's stories about the Caryaean and Persian prisoners.

Francesco was interested in illustrating both the basket and what was inside it. This interest pervades his discussions of other columns, all of which may be thought of as containing, and even sealing in (as if they were wicker sarcophagi), human figures. Indeed, when he discusses the fractional proportions of the human body, as illustrated by human-figure columns, he shows the skeleton that would be within the body that is within the shaft (figure 36). This strange conception, of a column as a mummy in a pyramidal basket, may have influenced Sebastiano Serlio when he designed the pair of swaddled herms in his treatise (figure 37). In both concep-

34
Francesco di Giorgio,
Origin of the Corinthian
order. From the Saluzziano
Codex, Biblioteca Reale,
Turin, folio 14v.

35
Francesco di Giorgio,
Colonna stolata. From the
Saluzziano Codex, folio
14v.

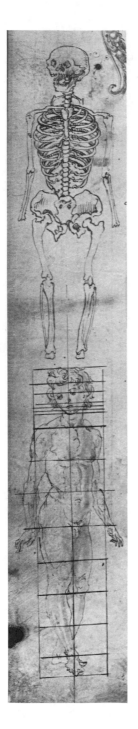

36
Francesco di Giorgio,
Skeleton. From the
Saluzziano Codex, folio
16v.

37
Sebastiano Serlio, Herms.
From *Livre extraordinaire de
Sebastien Serlio,* 1551.

tions the idea of figures imprisoned in order to perform an architectural function—to hold up a building—is clearly present. And that idea, of course, had pervaded Vitruvius's tales of the Caryatids and Persians. But it is also true that Francesco di Giorgio transforms Vitruvius's basket of goblets hidden by a bush on a tomb into a standing human body exactly like the standing bodies Vitruvius had taught us to see in Doric and Ionic columns.

He does something similar in his terminology. He translates into Italian Vitruvius's Greek terms, thus preserving, whether or not he was aware of their resonance, their references to personal ornament, body parts, and sacrificial elements such as bones, teeth, hair, and the like. But unlike Vitruvius he focuses each word and its corresponding architectural form around this image of the standing, imprisoned body. For example, on folio 21r of the Saluzziano copy of Francesco's treatise, which is a version of the book's earlier form, he illustrates a human face set within a full Ionic entablature (figure 38). Each feature is labeled: the upper corona, a crown of curling hair, is called the *ghola* (from the Latin *gula*, throat, but also appetite, ravenousness), by which is meant a cyma or S-curved molding. Although the most common meaning in Italian of *gola* is throat, it can also mean open circle or crown, which is precisely what Francesco, or his draughtsman, has drawn. Beneath this is the *strigia ovver regolo*, the comb or ruler, in this case a molding that ties the crown of hair. Then comes the *ghocciolatoio* or *corona*, the molding under which drops of water collect, located appropriately at the forehead and eyes; the *huovolo* or egg-zone, derived from the egg-and-claw or egg-and-dart molding of antiquity and here assimilated to the nose with, I gather, its oval nostrils and dart-like bridge; then the *dentello*, the row of teeth framed top and bottom by more *strigie*, which function this time as lips; then the *sottoghola* or *astragolo*. A *sottogola* is an underthroat, the area across the bottom of the jaws, and we saw that ἀστράγαλος meant necklace of bones or pearls, or small bones, here the chin. The throat proper is not another *gola* but the *fregio zoparo*, that is, *zoccolo*, the frieze, socle, or ζωοφόρος (the word Vitruvius uses), which means bringing forth living things, animal-bearing.[6] This is

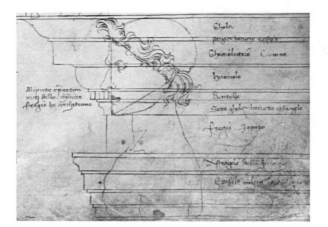

38
Francesco di Giorgio,
Entablature. From the
Saluzziano Codex, folio
21r.

more than appropriate, for sculptured fruits, flowers, and the like often appeared on Ionic and Corinthian friezes, though they do not appear in this sketch. Moreover, Ionic and Corinthian are both female orders, so in them this "throat" area could be appropriately decorated with necklaces and garlands. The next element is the *astragolo dell'architrave*, which comes at the point where the breastbone begins to curve outward. Translated into Vitruvian language Francesco's phrase could mean something like bone necklace on the main beam or trunk—a bead molding, that is, along a rafter or breast. (Note the English terms "chimney-breast," and "breastsummer.") In the entablature in another copy of the treatise,[7] the *huovolo* or egg-and-claw molding is actually called the *naso*, nose; the *dentello* becomes the *sottonaso*, undernose; and the *astragolo* becomes the *mento*, chin (figure 39).

In the later versions of his book Francesco develops gender differences between the orders, emphasizing and illustrating the delicacy and degree of ornament in Ionic and also illustrating, several times over, Vitruvius's parallel between Ionic volutes and women's hair. This time Vitruvius's story of the invention of the Corinthian

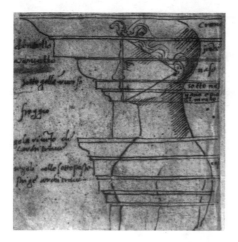

39
Francesco di Giorgio,
Entablature. From the
Beinecke Codex, Yale
University.

capital is correctly given. But though Francesco describes Callimachus's capital as a basket of goblets, he illustrates it as a young woman's face decorated with a double-horned, or voluted, egg-and-claw
crown topped by an abacus from which hang garlands of leaves
(figures 40, 41; we would call it today a Composite, not a Corinthian capital.)

With this drawing Francesco creates double tropes for *regole, co-
rone, dentelli,* and the like. On the surface, so to speak, these things
are elements of costume—combs, necklaces, and brooches. On a
second level they become lips, chins, and eyes. Only on a third level
do they emerge as architectural ornaments. The Corinthian girl's
basket is not supplanted by her head; rather, basket and head
merge, and then merge again into a third thing, an architectural
capital.

The names Francesco gives the parts of the capital continue the
troping process. The lowest element in the capitals in figures 40
and 41 is the beveled throat of the column top (*contractura, gola*);
the next is the *acroterio, balteo,* or *benda,* that is, summit, or shoulder
band or headband; topped by the *hypotrachelion* or upper neck or
torus; the *spira,* curl; the core of the capital, which is a tympanum
or drum; another *balteo* or shoulder band; *fusaroli* or more curls;

40
Francesco di Giorgio,
Head within capital. From
the Magliabecchiano
Codex, folio 33v.

41
Francesco di Giorgio,
"Corinthian" capital. From
the Magliabecchiano
Codex, folio 34r.

the ovolo or egg border; the echinus, which of course in Francesco's Italian lacks its Greek tropes of jar, sea urchin, hedgehog, vertebra, etc. The echinus in turn is protected by rings (*anelli*) and
triangular pins or arrows (*saggetti piramidali*), or what we call egg-
and-dart or (more sacrificially) egg-and-claw moldings. Finally,
there is the capital's astragal and gola, the throat with beaded or
boned rim. As a reminiscence of the original head of which the
capital is the architectural double trope, Francesco replaces (in figure 41) the woman's face with two rows of acanthus leaves. But two
caulicolae, or blossoms, gaze out from the capital, marking the
places where her eyes were. One recalls the Homeric hymn to De-
meter's "flower-faced girl," καλυκώπιδι κούρη (8). So here once
again he thinks of the head as being sealed within the acanthus
bush, a bit like Isabella's pot of basil in Boccaccio, which contains
her lover's head.

These treatises of Francesco di Giorgio are, as far as I know, the
first modern books to explore classical moldings systematically.
The impetus was clearly Francesco's fascination with their possibil-
ities for verbal and visual trope.

And one can go beyond this. In both the first and second treatise, the head and breast that form an entablature appear on the
following page, where they are extended so as to create Francesco's
familiar conception of a complete male figure inscribed within the
facade of a church (figure 42). This too is a Vitruvian touch, for it
comes out of his statement that the figure of a man with extended
legs and arms generates such perfect geometrical forms as a square
and a circle (3.1.2). One is familiar, also, with Francesco's delicate
little sketches of the city as a man, of a church plan formed the
same way, and of the plan of an apse derived from a human head.
His Vitruvian fancy even produces fortification plans whose case-
mate tunnels resemble a ring of dancing figurines (figure 43). One
thinks here of the ferocious Artemis dance at Patras. Under our
Vitruvian interpretation, then, these well-known drawings suggest
more than the oft-repeated idea that Francesco's architecture is an-
thropomorphic: they suggest buildings, and even whole towns,
made up of body *parts,* masses of overlapping, interpenetrating

88

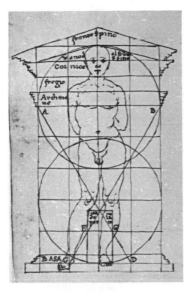

42
Francesco di Giorgio,
Church façade. From the
Magliabecchiano Codex,
folio 38v.

43
Francesco di Giorgio, Plan
of bastion. From the
Magliabecchiano Codex,
folio 64v.

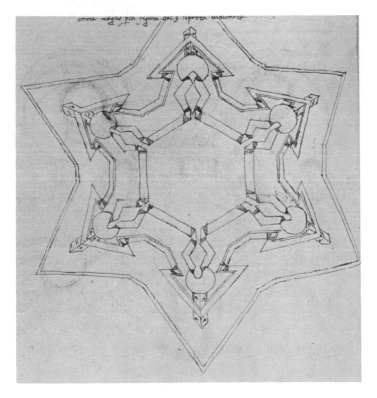

faces and torsoes—faces and torsoes decorated with, and merging with, ribbons, necklaces, curled hair, combs, and other ornaments. And, whether or not Francesco was conscious of their sacrificial nature, these fragments descend directly from the ones discussed in the first four chapters of this book.

Michelangelo

We have noted that medieval and early Renaissance caryatids seldom show signs of struggle. No more do Francesco's column-figures, though these latter do resemble bound prisoners. Yet Vitruvius makes a great point of the caryatids' and Persian captives' suffering under the weight of their porticoes. Justice done, and seen to be done, is the whole point of the stories.

In the Renaissance the most famous prisoners who may be seen as architectural supports are Michelangelo's *Captives* (figures 44–49). They were probably designed for the first, 1505, project for the tomb of Julius II and were begun two years after the second contract for the tomb was signed in 1513.[8] Unlike their medieval and Renaissance predecessors, these figures do suffer. Though few of them seem to be raising a superincumbent weight, they all strike poses that can be likened to antique support-figures such as those on the Olympaeum at Agrigento (figure 33). Most portray other aspects of prisonership: for example, they seem to have their hands bound behind their backs or behind their heads. All appear to be on exhibition, and they suit Vitruvius's phrases about a permanent procession of captives crushed by justice's revenge.[9] Let us note further that they are the earliest prisoners, at architectural scale, of the Renaissance and that the herms or human-headed pilasters they are bound to are the earliest Renaissance specimens of that form in an architectural setting.[10]

One might object here that Michelangelo's captives do not *comprise* columns, as do Vitruvius's Persians, but rather stand in front of pilasters. Yet this seeming discrepancy actually reinforces the link between the tomb of Julius and the Persian portico. In describing the latter monument, Pausanias says the statues of the Persians, of white marble, were ἐπὶ τῶν κιόνων. This *could* mean either that

44
Michelangelo, *Dying Slave*,
c. 1513–15. Musée du
Louvre, Paris.

45
Michelangelo, *Bound Slave*,
c. 1513–15. Musée du
Louvre, Paris.

46
Michelangelo, *Captive*,
1520s. Accademia,
Florence.

47
Michelangelo, *Captive*,
1520s. Accademia,
Florence.

48
Michelangelo, *Captive*,
1520s. Accademia.
Florence.

49
Michelangelo, *Captive*,
1520s. Accademia,
Florence.

the figures stood on top of the columns or that reliefs of Persians decorated the columns' surfaces. Yet the commonsense translation (ἐπὶ with the genitive) is that the statues were *in front of* the columns.[11] It cannot mean that the statues *were* the columns, as would be the case with true caryatids.[12]

Pausanias also says nothing of the Caryaean women and Persian men being portrayed in their clothes and ornaments, a fact of which Vitruvius makes much. Pausanias's reader is therefore free to assume that the statues on the Persian portico followed the fairly common custom in ancient art of representing prisoners nude.[13] The Sistine ceiling is alive with nude male figures who support architraves, many of them not unlike the tomb captives. Especially close are the infant caryatids in the sketch by Giacomo Rocchetti, after Michelangelo, for the 1505–13 project for the tomb (figure 50). And whether nude or clothed, many classical prisoners simply stand, as Michelangelo's do, in front of walls, columns, or trophies. There are for example those on the Roman arches at St.-Rémy and Carpentras (figure 51).[11] Other such prisoners, chained to trophies or herms like Michelangelo's, are found on Roman coins (figure 52).[15] Clement of Alexandria likens paganism itself to being tied to a statue "by the miserable chain of demon-worship" (*Protrepticon*, 1.7). In line with this tradition, a drawing in the Ashmolean for the bearded Boboli captive shows a true trophy, rather than a herm, behind the figure (figure 53).

Nonetheless one cannot assume that Pausanias completely replaces Vitruvius at this point. The latter's version of the tale was too well known for that. For one thing, in Vitruvius's tales the Doric and Ionic orders, and the caryatid and Persian porticoes as well, all represent social groups: they are Dorian soldiers, Ionian women, Caryaean women, Persian soldiers. Only the Corinthian capital represents an individual. In other words, the stories echo that Roman figural tradition in which sculptured human figures represent provinces, regions, towns, and the like.[16]

Could Michelangelo's figures for the tomb thus have been prisoners *and* provinces? In other words, could they have been captive provinces? By asking the questions I revive Vasari's claim that the

Captives personified "the provinces subjugated by [Julius] and made obedient to the Apostolic Church."[17] Against this it has been argued that in 1505, when the sculptures were most probably conceived, the pope had not yet "freed" a single foot of land.[18] This has pretty much squelched further discussion of Vasari's idea.

Yet it is not in fact the case that before 1503 Julius had subjugated, or as he would have put it, liberated no territory. Well before his election, indeed at the moment of Alexander VI Borgia's death, all the former papal cities that had been taken over by Cesare Borgia and occupied by Spanish troops reverted to Rome. The future pope, Giuliano della Rovere, at the time still bishop of Bologna, was one of the most active agents in this. The provinces returned to the Holy See were Cesena, Imola, Forlì, and several smaller Orsini and Colonna holdings.[19] After his election, the recapture of other former papal possessions formed the major political effort of Julius's papacy.

In 1507, two years after the first contract for the tomb, Egidio da Viterbo preached a sermon before Julius II.[20] Freed provinces are evoked again and again in this discourse, as in the repeated quotation from Isaiah 11.11: "The exiles of Israel shall come together, and the dispersed of Judea, from the four quarters of Earth." These exiles include Persians, that is, people of eastern lands, who gladly come, but also the unwilling: the *seditiosi* and *contumaces,* who will now be prisoners of the rule of God's Law. Julius will thus bring "unknown peoples" and "rebel cities" into the fold. He will appear in history as the *domitor ac subactor gentium impiarum,* the subduer and captor of the impious.[21]

At about this time, the Roman poet Giovanni Michele Nagoni addressed a congratulatory poem to the pope on the occasion of his reconquest of Bologna in 1506. In it Julius is adjured to reconquer the holy land. "Have mercy on the holy city of Jerusalem," the poet writes, "the enslaved city, dressed in mourning and flowing with tears, asks particularly for your help, your protection, your power, your military expertise. Who, except Julius, would presume to extricate Antioch, Ptolemaic Alexandria, and Jerusalem, the workshop of our salvation, from the teeth of the barbarians? Who

50
Jacomo Rocchetti, after
Michelangelo, 1505 project
for tomb of Julius II.
Kupferstichkabinett,
Staatliche Museen, Berlin.

51
Carpentras, Roman arch,
prisoner reliefs. (Photo:
Art Resource)

52
Roman coin with prisoner
tied to trophy. From
Bonner Jahrbücher, 120,
1911.

53
Michelangelo or assistant,
Slaves tied to trophies.
Ashmolean Museum,
Oxford.

but Julius would dare to carry the sign of the cross to the Euphrates and the Tigris and restore to Mesopotamia a Christian name?" The frontispiece of the manuscript of this poem in the Vatican Library, be it noted, is illustrated with bound prisoners being freed by Julius.[22]

I believe that these phrases explain the original signification of Michelangelo's *Captives*.[23] The possibility that Michelangelo's figures were for a Persian portico is reinforced when we note that the odd pose of one of the Persian captives in Cesariano's 1521 Vitruvius (figure 67) is a reversal of that of one of Michelangelo's prisoners (figure 46). Further reinforcement for their being geographical entities is that the main Renaissance source for Michelangelo's sculptures, the figures by Antonio Federighi on a holy-water basin in the Siena Cathedral (figure 54), represent the four parts of the earth.[24] Egidio in fact speaks of the pope's liberations as taking place throughout the *quatuor universi partes* that are still in bondage to idolatry.[25] One recalls that Michelangelo was also reviving the use of the herm for the first time in the Renaissance, and that in antiquity herms had had a strongly geographical and territorial meaning.

Furthermore, one of the most famous sets of statues to derive from Michelangelo's 1505–13 tomb project, the *omenoni* of Leone Leoni's house in Milan, also represents provinces and/or prisoners (figure 55).[26] And, as Michael Mezzatesta points out, the *omenoni* have an equal debt to the Persian portico illustrated in Daniele Barbaro's edition of Vitruvius (figure 56).[27] In short, Michelangelo's famous *Captives* may be read as a Christianized redaction of the Spartan portico. But, appropriately, the pagan mood of eternal punishment is replaced by the idea of eventual freedom. For those who object that not all the *Captives* are in poses suggesting architectural support, I point to the putto-caryatids in the Sistine ceiling, whose poses are so very close to those of the *Captives*, and all of whom are unquestionably *Stutzfiguren*.

54
Antonio Federighi, Holy-
water stoup, begun
1482(?). Cathedral, Siena.

Let us return now to Francesco di Giorgio. We saw him identi-
fying various moldings as teeth, noses, hair, ribbons, and the like,
based on Vitruvius's nomenclature. Francesco, unlike Vitruvius,
draws these moldings both in their abstract and concrete human
forms. Yet for Francesco the analogy of moldings with body fragments is only a didactic device. Michelangelo carries out the analogy in a finished work of architecture, the New Sacristy of San
Lorenzo. The upper molding of the dado running behind the
tombs consists of a row of egg-and-claw ornaments crowning a row
of dentils (figure 57). The eggs are broken open, in the usual way,
to reveal the yolk or κόκκος that the Greeks identified with the soul
of a future creature.

Below this, Michelangelo has reread the molding in terms of its
visual tropes. That is, he turns the eggshell, a *conca d'uova*, into a
seashell, *conchiglia*. This in turn becomes a helmet. The yolk meanwhile turns into a full-grown human, a face with scowling eyes and
shouting maw. The dentils or teeth are the maw's tusks. The face's
cheeks turn into mustaches that flow down into curls outside the
rim of the shell-helmet and meet the points of the claws, which are

55
Antonio Abondio,
Prisoner, c. 1565. Casa
degli Omenoni, Milan.

PROEMIO.

re i tronchi di spoglie hostili per segno, & ricordanza della vittorie, quel tronco adorno così, chiamansi trofeo, come in più luoghi si vede nella historia di Thucydide, volendo i Lacedemonij havere memoria della bella impresa, che fecero sotto Pausania contra i Persi non vollero alzare, & adornare i Trofei, ma fecero cosa più illustre, & memorabile, come dice Vitr. fabricando un portico con i denari tratti delle vendute spoglie, chi si dicono, manubie, & della pr[·]che e tutto il corpo del bottino, di questo portico ne fa mentione il dotto Pausania ne i Laconici, dice ancho nell'Attica ragionando, della stirpe di Pausania, e pone la genealogia di quello, & nell'Archadia dice che Pausania figliuolo di Cleombroto Duce de Platesi hebbe impedimento dalle ribalderie che egli poi fece, di esser chiamato benemerito della Grecia, Dalle historie adunque occasione prende l'Architetto di adornare l'opere sue, come ancho Vitr. in molti luoghi adorna i suoi volumi, come nel Vl. cap. del primo, nel I X. del secondo, nel primo del VI. & in tutti i proemi de i suoi. X. libri, & altrove è pieno di belli ammaestramenti tratti dalle historie.

56
Daniele Barbaro, Persian
portico. From *Vitruvius*,
1556.

now also exaggerated into realistic weapons with long prongs.[28] Clearly, these once again are warriors, though not necessarily Persian ones, who have been forced into service as architectural supports.

A drawing at Windsor, attributed to Michelangelo and in any case based on his ideas, develops these creatures into a more finished head (figure 58). Here the helmet becomes a rayed crown (*corona*—another molding), the hair and mustache are more wildly curled, and the tongue is now as prominent as the teeth.

Only slightly less well known are Michelangelo's sketches for the pilaster bases of the Medici Chapel. In the one in the Casa Buonarroti, inscribed in the artist's hand, beak moldings predominate (figure 59).[29] Francesco di Giorgio calls these shapes *trochili,* from the Latin *trochilus,* plover, wren (whence presumably the idea of the beak).[30] The trochili are separated in Michelangelo's sketch by what Francesco calls *scozie,* scotias or shades, which as we have seen are associated with the goddess Scotia and with σκότος, darkness, death; and here we may also add σκώπτω, mocking, jeering, scoffing. Michelangelo might or might not have known this Greek word, but he certainly knew the Italian words for tongue, tooth, beak, egg, and the like, which at least from Francesco's time were used for these moldings.

Michelangelo seems to have troped architectural and other names on one further occasion. The Porta Pia, Rome, 1561–64, was commissioned by Giovanni Angelo Medici of Milan, Pius IV (not one of the Florentine Medici).[31] On its facade are two paterae surmounted by stole-like motifs with fringes (figure 60). Ciceroni, ancient and modern, have often described these as the basins and towels associated in the Renaissance with *medici*—barber-surgeons.[32] This they may well be, and if so they are already parodistic; yet the existence of *paterae* commissioned by the *pater,* pope, should not be neglected, nor should the fact that the fringes of the towels are formed of Michelangelo's characteristic pyramidal guttae. In this case the architectural "drops," as Armando Schiavo points out, would be dripping from the barber's towels.[33] It is the same conceit we saw in the Doric frieze (figure 15).

57
Michelangelo, Details of
moldings, 1520s, Medici
Chapel, San Lorenzo,
Florence.

58
Michelangelo (?), Study for
mask. Royal Library,
Windsor. Reproduced by
gracious permission of Her
Majesty the Queen.

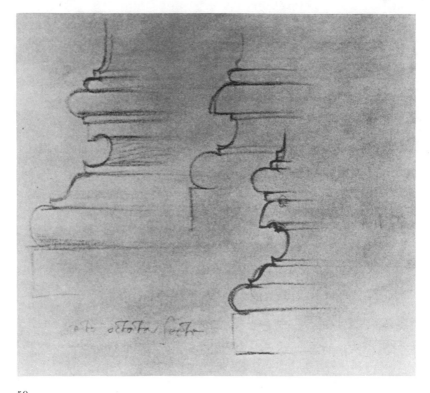

59
Michelangelo, Design for
pilaster base in the Medici
Chapel. Casa Buonarroti,
Florence.

60
Michelangelo, Porta Pia,
Rome, 1561–64. (Photo:
Alinari)

Raphael

Alberti, Filarete, and Francesco di Giorgio all write independent treatises rather than commentaries on Vitruvius, though their treatises are clearly indebted to him. The next phase is one of Vitruvius editions, beginning with the *editio princeps,* Rome, 1486, and continuing with Fra Giocondo's illustrated edition of 1511. As far as I know this contains the first attempt to illustrate the caryatids and the Persian portico (figures 61, 62) in a Vitruvius text, though it postdates the first projects for the Julius tomb.

Fra Giocondo shows the caryatids in their *stolae* or long garments, presumed to be characteristic of Roman matrons, and standing on Attic bases (perhaps reflecting Vitruvius's simile between Ionic bases and sandals in 4.1.7). Their hands are folded before them, which makes them look a bit like prisoners in the stocks. Their hats, which support the load, are possible versions of Vitruvius's ἐπιϰράνατα, which means kerchief but also column capital (Euripides, *Iphigeneia in Tauris,* 51).[34] The Persian portico makes an only slightly Orientalized twin for the caryatid group. The figures in both porticoes have the impassivity of the traditional *Stützfiguren,* though they illustrate the very passage in which such a point is made of the statues' bearing an almost insupportable weight.

A few years later, another event occurred that increased Vitruvus's importance on the Roman scene. Raphael, on succeeding Fra Giocondo as architect of St. Peter's, commissioned one of the first two Italian translations of the Latin text.[35] It might have seemed an auspicious moment for Vitruvius studies: there were also Raphael's famous letter to Leo X on ancient Rome and his various projected buildings *all'antica,* such as the Villa Madama. And when he was investigating the possibility of rebuilding Rome, Raphael wrote in a much-quoted letter to Baldassarre Castiglione: "I would like to recover the beautiful forms of the ancient buildings but don't know if this is a flight of Icarus. The illumination Vitruvius offers me is great but not enough."[36] This would especially be the case since Raphael, under Bramante's influence, was trying to revive Roman imperial vaulted architecture, whereas Vitruvius, who

61
Fra Giocondo, Caryatid
portico. From *Vitruvius,*
1511.

died before that architecture came into existence, was looking at
the essentially trabeated and columnar modes of Roman Republi-
can and Greek temple architecture.[37]

Nonetheless, as a painter if not as an architect, Raphael may
have gained illumination from Vitruvius and his Renaissance followers. I would like to propose that, since Raphael in c. 1515 was
embarking on an architectural career, and since he had commissioned a translation of Vitruvius, he also looked at Francesco's treatise. After all, Francesco was not just a fantasist but a respected

62
Fra Giocondo, Persian
portico. From *Vitruvius*,
1511.

practical builder with considerable experience in Raphael's native
Urbino.[38] In any event the two artists seem to have an unnoticed
affinity. It is a commonplace of art-historical interpretation that
Raphael makes architectural "temples" in his paintings. Thus John
Pope-Hennessy in a much-made comparison contrasts Perugino's
Marriage of the Virgin (Musée, Caen) with Raphael's version of the
scene in Milan and shows that Raphael's group forms an apse-like
structure while Perugino's does not.[39] Even more architectural, of
course, is the grouping of figures in the *Disputà* (figure 63). Here

63
Raphael, *Disputà*, 1511–15.
Vatican, Rome. (Photo. Art
Resource)

we see an altar and steps, surmounted by seated, standing, and floating figures. Above the jagged, active disarray of the earthly priests and preachers who form the ground floor of this edifice is a smooth semicircle of cloud. On it, as in a clerestory, sit the Fathers of the Church and other saints in perfect order. They resemble seated statues that have been deprived of their surrounding niches and wall. They are close in date, style, and pose, to Michelangelo's Sistine prophets and sibyls and, more importantly for us, to the Moses for the tomb of Julius II.[40] It has been suggested that the two circles of figures represent the Church Militant on earth imitating the Church Triumphant in Heaven and that the phrase "on earth, as it is in Heaven" is being invoked.[41] The huge circular gold nimbus behind the group of Christ, the Virgin, and Saint John functions as a window in this figure-formed apse, while the dome is made up of floating angels and rays that spread from its apex like the ribs of a true architectural dome. Indeed, one could say that here Raphael adapts Francesco di Giorgio's ultra-Vitruvian anthropomorphism to the requirements of a Roman vaulted style.[42]

In the Neoplatonic atmosphere that bathed these works when they were created, it is not difficult to read Raphael's "temple" as an eternal prototype, as the Church as a communion of saints. But Renaissance Vitruvianism is clearly responsible for the fact that the idea now takes the literal form of an apsidal chapel, reminiscent of the original scheme for a Cappella Giulia and, with its curved banks of benches flanking the altar, even more reminiscent of Antonio da Sangallo the Younger's sketch for the remodeling of the chancel of Santa Maria sopra Minerva (figure 64).[43] We can attribute to the same influence the fact that human and superhuman figures constitute Raphael's columns, entablature, and dome.

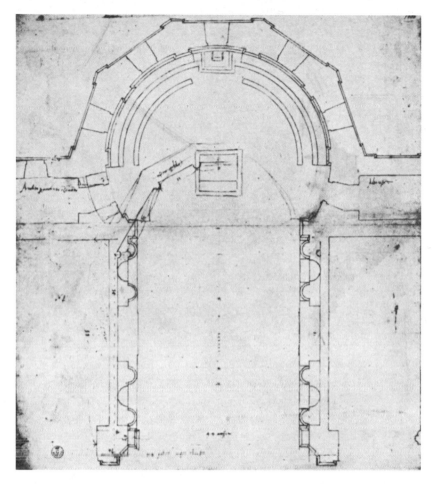

64
Antonio da Sangallo the
Younger, Sketch for
remodeling the chancel of
Santa Maria sopra
Minerva, Rome. Uffizi,
Florence, A1313.

6

Cesariano, The *Vitruvius Teutsch*, and Sambin

Cesare Cesariano

Cesare Cesariano's Italian Vitruvius, the first fully illustrated and annotated edition of that author, appeared in 1521. In it Cesare revives the notion that an entablature is a massing together of animal parts and sacrificial gear. Also, more than any previous architectural writer, including even Vitruvius himself, Cesare is concerned that his readers know the Greek names of ornamental forms. And where Vitruvius does not explain these names when he uses them (their meanings and associations were known to his original readers), Cesare does. Thus Cesare defines the *caulicolae* at the corners of the Corinthian capital, which we have said were sprays or stalks (and which Francesco di Giorgio troped visually as the dead Corinthian girl's eyes), as καυλοί (in Homer, spear shafts *or* stalks; see figure 12), that is, part of a spear or sword; but Cesare also says it means the human penis and the thyrsus (a wand tipped with a pine cone, ivy, vine leaves, or the like, used in Bacchic rites). Similarly, he defines βάσις as *gradum, gressionem, firmamentum, depositionem.*[1] Here is another bouquet of tropes: step, stepping, support, depositing.[2]

The same thing happens when, discussing the origins of the Ionic order, Cesare speaks of volutes and moldings as different kinds of hair or *cincini*, or of fruit, *encarpi*. Vitruvius's words are *cimatiis* and *encarpis*. In Cesare they become the echinus of the Ionic capital and festoons of fruit (figure 10). Both are once again Greek; κῦμα, the base of κυμάτιον, is billow, but also cauliflower stalk, while καρπός is fruit. In Cesare the *cimatio* is not just a cyma molding but the fronds and decorations that the young wear in their hair. And he links καρπός to words meaning fruit-bearing or fructifying, as if the fruit in architectural ornament had ripened in place.

But it is in his discussion of the birth of the orders that Cesare is most original. He discusses these tales more fully than any earlier (or later) commentator, and the stories of the Caryaeans and Persians play a prominent role. In Vitruvius the theme of public justice, expressed by Caryaean and Persian stories, is more or less separate from the ancestral theme in the Doric and Ionic stories. In Cesariano the two themes fuse.[3]

The fusion occurs because, for Cesariano, the founding of communities is expressed architecturally in the exhibition of justice accomplished, that is, punishment. Such exhibitions are not proposed for individuals but for groups. According to Cesariano, in peace and war, in justice or treachery, the Greeks always acted in groups. When wartime treachery occurred, as it often did, group punishment was inflicted on the offenders by the next generation as a group. That is what happens with the Caryaeans. They are traitors who must be displayed to later generations "in order that the punishment of the sin of the Caryaean women might be known to posterity and historically recorded" (Vitruvius, 1.1.5). Cesare explains that the women's *stolae* (figure 65) are symbols of their marriage contracts to Caryaean men, that is to say of the loyalties that should have made them prefer death to being the concubines of the Persian invaders. Their crime was the greater, he adds, in that the Caryaeans were by nature proud and undefeated. The Greeks held this people to be stronger and more intelligent than any other nation. The weight of the structure on their heads, meanwhile, is linked to the fact that the ancients meted out punishments in terms of the monetary weight of the crime being punished (Cesariano on Vitruvius, 1.5).

In the Persian portico (figure 66), the captured satraps form the lowest part, bear the greatest weight, and stand upright on plinths inscribed with what I take to be their names. Directly above are wearied soldiers in full armor supporting an entablature whose frieze is decorated with cups and goblets (F, G). On the right, in an alternative version, kneeling soldiers support a huge trophy-laden

65
Cesare Cesariano, Caryatid
portico. From *Vitruvius*,
1521.

66
Cesare Cesariano, Persian
portico. From *Vitruvius*,
1521.

section of entablature (labeled DEKH).[4] They seem about to be devoured by its bared dentils. The soldiers each have one hand between these fangs. The darts of an egg-and-dart molding also point down at them. Above the soldiers, bust-length Persian captives grasp Ionic volutes resembling horned headdresses. The frieze of swords, chains, crowns, bowls, and goblets is meanwhile interrupted by carved brackets supporting smaller kneeling soldiers. The whole design richly memorializes the defeat of these prisoners by the portico's Greek builders. As Cesare makes clear, it is an object lesson both to later generations of would-be invaders (note that the inscriptions are in Persian) and to the Spartans themselves—a monument, in short, to the ancestral victory that secured Greek independence. The experience of looking at the Persian portico, says Cesare, should be like that of Aeneas when he interpreted reliefs of the deeds of his ancestors on the temple of Juno at Carthage. "Here, too," says Aeneas, "virtue has its due rewards; here, too, misfortune and mortal sorrows touch the heart" (*Aeneid*, 1.435ff.).

This is why Cesariano's caryatids and Persians, unlike all earlier such *Stützfiguren* except Michelangelo's *Captives*, suffer. Indeed, as noted, some of Cesare's Persians strike poses possibly influenced by Michelangelo (figure 67); though we should note that only the two finished *Captives* (figures 44, 45) surely date from before the publication of Cesariano's book. In any event, it begins to look as if Michelangelo and Cesariano were privy to this Vitruvian insight.

Cesare goes to great lengths to show that the Caryaean and Persian porticoes are linked to the establishment of Doric and Ionic. He says that Caryae, home of the Caryatids, was the same place as the Caria where the Doric and Ionic orders were born.[5] He adds, moreover, that the first Ionic columns were full-fledged statue-columns of matrons. Only later did architects gradually simplify the shafts of these columns, says Cesare, eventually forming only the capitals into human heads. In this way a herm, term, or other human-headed stele is a way-station in the process by which the caryatid developed into the column. Finally, he says, even the heads became ordinary capitals. (Let us note that here Cesare is

67
Cesare Cesariano, Persian
column. From *Vitruvius*,
1521.

composing a variant on Francesco di Giorgio's idea that columns contain hidden human bodies.) Examples of the process, says Cesare, are found in San Lorenzo Maggiore, Milan, which he says was built from the remains of a temple of Hercules. He may have had in mind the battered Corinthian capitals of the Roman colonnade now reassembled in front of the church (figure 68), some of which do look a bit like human heads.[6] Anyway, the columns in Cesare's diagram (figure 65) marked L, R, and H are other specimens of the development.

A similar process occurred, says Cesare, in the development of wooden architecture. And here we return to our discussion of sacred trees and sacred-tree columns. Once again the earliest supports were statues of human beings that later generations of builders gradually redesigned as abstract supports. Thus the raised arms of wooden caryatids became diagonal braces. But the braces, Cesare points out, retained their names and continued to be called *brachioli*, arms, in Italian. Thus for Cesare both stone and wooden columns—and not just in temples but in houses as well— are abstract statues. In these cases, however, the columns are the ancestors themselves, not the foes of those ancestors.

Yet the notion of the column as a prisoner is not absent from this part of Cesare's discussion. He here reinserts a notion we have so often looked at earlier, that of the bound figure, of the support constrained to its work. He claims that the original wooden houses of the Greeks were supported by tree-columns (*arboreae columne*) rising from their roots as Nature had made them, and that the spreading of the trunks at root and branch level expressed the burden of the roof they perpetually sustained. To counteract the spreading of the post's base, the ends were strengthened with bindings. The bronze capitals and bases one sometimes sees on marble columns, says Cesare, are the descendants of these. Other architects, sensing that wood is easily split lengthwise, bound the whole trunk at regular intervals with bands called *mutules, mensole,* or *calastrelli*. These are also to be found on pilasters and engaged columns. Or, he tells us, such trunks can be ornamented as telamones. He does not add the appropriate fact that in Greek τελαμῶνες were

68
Milan, San Lorenzo
Maggiore, Roman
colonnade.

both colossal male figures used as columns and straps or bindings. This trope, however, could be responsible for Serlio's encased gate-keepers in figure 37.

Such bindings, says Cesare, should be inscribed with brief memorable sayings, like the names of the Caryaean women and Persian warriors shown in Cesare's plate. He says these things are still visible in ordinary houses in the town of Mutina and that the Greeks, like the Romans, erected monumental inscribed columns to commemorate military events (Cesariano on Vitruvius, 1.1). Caryatids, prisoners, herms, terms, atlantes, and Doric, Ionic, and Corinthian columns were set up as freestanding monuments throughout the Roman empire, presumably as monuments to the ancestral justice done against treachery. One might call them trophies of the battle against civil disorder. This practice, says Cesare, constituted a form of public instruction known as stylography—literally, teaching or demonstrating via columns.[7] Thus Cesare would seem to view even the columns of Trajan and Marcus Aurelius as "hidden" or metaphorical colossal statues wrapped in bindings.

Vitruvius had implied that Doric and Ionic were the father and mother of Corinthian. Cesariano develops this idea of procreative activity among columns. He prints a diagram of what he calls the six "generations" of columns (figure 69). There are "the Doric column first imitated from the male body," as in Vitruvius; then comes a female Doric column, a matron one diameter higher, and more ornate, than the male. She is given, as an alternative to her normal head, a garland-and-face capital. Next there is the Ionic column, laden with necklaces and earrings but unfluted. The Corinthian column, in turn, is properly a virgin, though we have seen that Cesare says its caulicolae or upper spirals come from the word for penis, καυλὸς. Then comes another novelty, the "Attigurgan [*scil.* Ἀττικουργὴς, 'wrought in the Attic fashion'] column, a straight-sided pilaster or anta whose shaft is a weapon frieze or trophy. Meanwhile the Tuscan column [is] laid out in its normal proportions, with ornament, which can in accordance with other customs have channels, *exochis* [from ἐχοτεία, channeled] and *metochis*." In Greek a μέτοχος is a partner, so possibly Cesare means that these columns can be coupled (a rare practice in his period). Above all, these columns have fanciful capitals, with heads, griffins, human figures, and the like.

The Vitruvius Teutsch

In 1549 a German book based on Vitruvius was published. Many of its plates are inspired by Cesare's, but other plates, and the text, carry Renaissance thinking about statue-columns into new areas. The historical development from statue to column posited by Cesare is now illustrated in thirteen plates. What is proposed, however, is not simply the gradual abstracting of human form. Rather, the transformation takes place through the shuffling of plants, ornaments, and body fragments—not only of humans but of animals—into new and strange arrays. This process, which is without true precedent among antique *Stützfiguren*,[8] had only been foreshadowed in Francesco di Giorgio and Cesariano.

The *Vitruvius Teutsch* illustrates many more types of ancient sup-

69
Cesare Cesariano, The
orders of architecture.
From *Vitruvius*, 1521.

port figure than are mentioned by Vitruvius. Besides the caryatid there is the herm, the term or Terminus, the Atlas or atlante, and the telamon (see chapter 5 and Vitruvius, 6.7.6). A herm, we have seen, is a Hermes image in which the god's head, or head and chest, grow out of a stele. They carry all the associations of Hermes himself. Herms appear over graves to mark out sacred ground and because Hermes, as the psychopomp, or conductor of shades in the underworld, will care for the deceased. As the god of borders it is he who leads the soul across the border of death. More fundamentally, a ἕρμα is a foundation, a prop, even a pile of stones.[9]

A term, τέρμα, boundary, end, destiny, and trope of herm, is another boundary marker, of similar form, but portraying Terminus, a Roman god of boundaries, zones, and terminations.[10] An atlante is of course named after Atlas, who holds the lofty columns separating earth from the heavens. Atlas's name is rich in poetic tropes. Ἄτλας is a god (*Odyssey*, 1.52) or Titan, and his name tropes those of the Atlantic and of the fabulous island of Atlantis. Thus atlantes suggest support of the heavens, the distant, the fantastic, and the colossal (see Vitruvius, 6.7.6). The figures who supported the roof of the temple at Agrigento were Atlases (figure 33), and their multiplication here suggests that the entablature and tympanum of that temple were conceived as models of heaven itself. But less sublime atlases exist. The neck vertebra (or echinus) that directly supports the human skull is called the Atlas.[11] Other tropes would be ἄθλαστος, that which cannot be crushed, and ἀθλεύω, contend for a prize, be a combatant or athlete.[12]

Telamones were other forms of Atlantes. Their name also means a strap, the base of a stele, and any sort of bandage or wrapping. We can think here of Francesco di Giorgio's *colonne stolate* (figure 35) and Cesare's idea that all columns are bound bodies.

With some of these new terms we enter the realm of the divine. Atlas, Hermes, and Terminus are gods. They and their columnar images were sacrificed to, hung with wreaths, doused with wine and honey, given gifts, prayed over. The images were equipped with altars, votive tablets, and the like. In *Fasti* Ovid says that when the Capitol in Rome was being built, the whole company of the gods withdrew, except for Jupiter, to make room for Terminus (2.667ff.). His former task had been to keep the different gods' sanctuaries separate, but now he was to mark out the temenos (note the trope) of *the* god, Jupiter. For this reason Terminus's image stood in Jupiter's Capitoline temple—Jupiter, who rules the whole world, and whose sanctuary, whose empire, has therefore *no* boundaries. The same is after all true of Rome itself: *Romanae spatium est urbis et orbis idem:* the boundary of Rome is that of the city and that of the world. No wonder the popes appropriated Ovid's slogan. It was perfect, for instance, for Julius II. Hence Atlas, Hermes, and Terminus bridge the gap between a column, which may represent an ancestral votary or ancestral justice, and a temple image, which portrays a god proper.

Dionysius of Helicarnassos (*Roman Antiquities,* 3.69) tells another tale about Terminus. He says that when Tarquin wanted to purge the Capitoline of all divinities, he was successful with all but this god, who could take any form, human, animal, or vegetable or, especially, all three. In short he could be a composite monster, a concretion of heads, thighs, flowers, and bones. The other figures we have discussed—the Atlases, the columns, the caryatids—like the temples with which they were associated, might be draped, bound, hung with such offerings. But Terminus could actually *be comprised* of such things.

This is a great difference, responsible for the wide efflorescence in Europe of a type of support figure we have not yet looked at. The phenomenon has been well studied by Erik Forssmann and Georg Weise, and I need not repeat what they say.[13] Yet while these authors supply an abundance of bizarre columns and monstrous caryatids, they nowhere explain their origins. They isolate a corpus of objects, well defined in time and distribution, but make little attempt to suggest a meaning. A look at the *Vitruvius Teutsch,* in the context of what we have been saying in this book, will throw new light on the problem (figure 70).

Here, first of all, we see Terminus variously as a swaddled bush

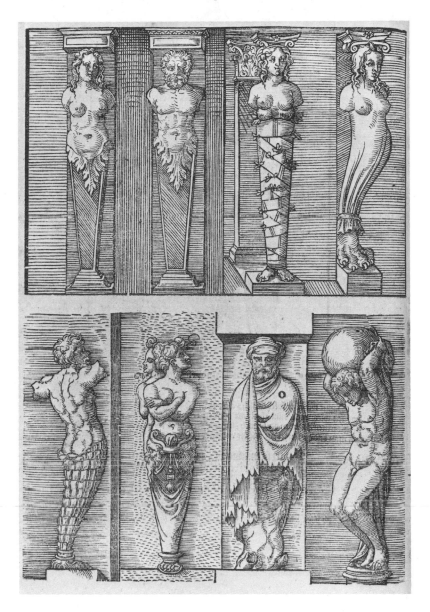

70
Caryatids, herms, and
atlantes. From *Vitruvius
Teutsch,* 1548.

topped by a four-breasted armless woman (suggesting Francesco di Giorgio's rereading of the Callimachus story, figure 34); as an armless woman with a lion's foot; as an armless merman; as a two-bodied female, girded with mascherons and with a single foot; and as an Atlas grown from an undoubtedly sacred tree trunk. Armlessness was a greek metaphor for harmlessness (to use a trope valid in English but not in Greek), for it was the custom to remove the arms of a slain enemy and set them under his body so as to evade the vengeance of his spirit. This made him a sacrifice to the gods. μασχαλίζω means "I put under the armpits," that is, put the severed arms under the body or, alternatively, string them along with his nose, ears, and other appendages, around his neck (Aeschylus, *Choephori*, 439). Thus Terminus may have evaded identification. Yet when we see him in architecture, he has been identified and endures the punishment of being forced to support a building like a caryatid, holding aloft an entablature and, as god of boundaries, marking out the zone of a bay. I have earlier referred to ἀποτυμπάνοντοι, that is, the prisoners who were shown off, imprisoned beneath the tympanum. We may attribute this role to Terminus. Like a caryatid or a Persian column, a term is a protean force that has been captured and put to architectural use.

The illustrator of the *Vitruvius Teutsch* is also one of the rare artists who displays the Caryaean women in the attitudes of suffering, or at least of penitential meditation, that Vitruvius specifies (figure 71). Examples of the same thing in actual architecture are rare. One is in the tomb of Giovanni Pesaro (1699) by Baldassare Longhena and Melchior Barthel in the Frari, Venice. Another is the careyatid portico now in the Vierschaar in the Amsterdam Town Hall, 1651–54, by Artus Quellinus and his workshop.

Hugues Sambin

The architectural exhibition of these monstrous shapes was reinforced, more in France than elsewhere, by the new science of teratology, the study of monsters and deformed beings. The great French physician Ambroise Paré was a key contributor to this lit-

71
The women of Caryae.
From *Vitruvius Teutsch,*
1548.

erature. Like other books on teratology, Paré's (1573) stresses the need to interpret monsters as messages from God, or from the gods.[14] As with ancient sacrifices, so with monsters, ancient or modern—the properly prepared investigator can see in them prodigies, warnings about current or future events. Paré revives the theme of sacrificial transformations between human and beast, and between human, beast, and plant. For example, when the inhabitants of Ravenna, not wishing to be liberated by the French from Venetian rule, basely fought off the invading army of Louis XII, God punished them by causing their newborns to appear legless, armless, or otherwise monstrous. Monsters can make more general social statements, too: when sodomites mate with atheists, for example, the result is children with dogs' legs. Paré even considers whether God, or the gods, might transform humans entirely or partly into animals as a form of punishment. And might not Ovid, he asks, whose characters are punished by being turned into trees, rocks, or animals, be telling literal truths?

The nightmarish columns of the *Vitruvius Teutsch* and of parallel works, such as the books by Wendel Dietterlin and Vredeman de Vries, go hand in hand with the writings of magicians like Hieronymus Cardanus and philosophers like Pietro Pomponazzi.[15] Cardanus in 1556 tells us in a book entitled *De la subtilité* that the kingdom of fauna on earth corresponds to that of the fauna of the sea. He instances dogs, elephants, men, and women on the one hand, and on the other dogfish, elephant fish, the triton, and the nereid (he assumes the existence of such beings). Their monstrosity is a tribute to Nature's abundance and creativity, her infinite combinatorial powers.[16] Such things should be accepted and celebrated, he says, putting into words the sentiment that explains the appearance of monsters in the architecture of these times.

The theme of justice is ever-present. Like caryatids and Persian warriors, monsters are examples of justice done. Pomponazzi, like Paré, attributes the advent of monsters to God's discontent with human behavior and to the influence of the stars. When earthly bodies misbehave, heavenly bodies punish them. The tropes of "monster" are all present to make the point: *monstranda sunt, de-*

monstrant, demonstrantur, they are to be shown, they show, and they are shown.

All this explains why Renaissance herms and terms are so special. Compared to the monsters of ancient art, those of the sixteenth and seventeenth centuries are monstrosities indeed. Antiquity has composite creatures, of course—centaurs, taurocephali, and the like—and the sort of superabundance we see in the Ephesian Artemis with her many breasts. One can also see virtuoso combinatorial powers in Cerberus, the many-headed dog of Hades, or in Apollodorus's Typhon: "As far as his thighs he was of human shape . . . and from [each hand] projected a hundred dragons' heads. From the thighs downward he had huge coils of vipers . . . his body was all winged: unkempt hair streamed on the wind from his head and cheeks" (*The Library,* 1.6.3). But in ancient art such creatures are pretty tame compared to their Renaissance successors.

This interest in monsters was much apparent in architectural treatises. Weird assemblages of human and animal body parts, of architectural foliage both abstract and naturalistic, teem in books such as Heinrich Vogtherr's *Ein frembds und wunderbars Kunstbüchlin allen Molern, Bildschnitzen, Goldschmiden . . .* , Strassburg, 1537; Jan Vredeman de Vries's *Caryatidum (vulgus termas vocat),* Antwerp, 1560; Joseph Boillot's *Nouveaux pourtraitz et figures de termes pour user en architecture,* Langres, 1592; Gabriel Kramer's *Architecture von den fünf Saülen sambt ihren Ornamenten und Zierden aus dem Jahre 1600,* Frankfurt-am-Main, 1595; and Daniel Meyer's *Architecture oder Verzeichnuss allerhand Eynfassungen an Thüren, Fenstern und Decken . . .* , Frankfurt-am-Main, 1609.

One example of this new degree of monstrosity in architectural thought is a book by Hugues Sambin: *De la diversité des termes,* Lyon, 1572.[17] Sambin's plates map a progression. There are eighteen pairs, male and female. Six different architectural orders are represented—Tuscan, Doric, Ionic, Corinthian, Composite (part Ionic, part Corinthian), and Supercomposite. The latter mixes all five previous orders. The Tuscan is the most primitive; indeed it is subhuman. The Supercomposite is the most advanced, and is superhuman. The orders in between map stages in this progression. The lower orders—and here that phrase can be used literally—are humanoid figures emerging from mossy stones or ruined masonry. Above these are captives, bound and armless. Above these, priestly or divine torsoes rise over altars, often grasping lambs, goats, and the like. Men, women, and animal victims are often horned and crowned with garlands of fruit and flowers, or dressed in bucrania. The highest level is that of the multibodied monster who combines altar, victims, altar image of the divinity, and, rising above, the form of the multiple-headed priest or priestess who conducts the sacrifice.

The male in the first pair (figure 72) emerges from a tall cone of rock, as befits a basement or sub-basement support. From this rises the naked, Michelangelesque torso of an armless, bearded peasant. His head supports the weight of a heavy, rusticated keystone. His stony chest and shoulders sprout weeds and drooping grasses. His mate (figure 73) is also naked, except that the rocky cone from which she emerges forms a sort of skirt, and her head is wrapped in a kerchief. The woman's rocky support is overgrown with more rapacious weeds than her husband's. A snake and a salamander occupy it. In Sambin the Tuscan order receives an ancestral meaning and becomes the most primal and chthonic of the architectural orders.

I will skip over the gradual transformations and turn to Sambin's seventh pair (figures 74, 75). Once again the two figures are armless, are sacrificed victims. Now the male is horned and bearded, bent beneath a vine-decked Doric entablature and fruited keystone, from which a horned human head emerges. This somber, black-browed satyr is bound at chest, knee, and ankle by thick belts. So he is a telamon as well as a herm. A mantle hangs behind, disguising to some extent his armless state. The female Doric term, also a satyr, has the same configuration as her mate. In both, the feet form a column base, the toe-knuckles create an astragal, the drapery is fluting, the fetters are shaft bands, and the head, with its horns and curly masses of hair, forms the capital.

The tenth pair consists of a vigorous, richly caparisoned Ionic couple (figures 76, 77), once again armless. They support their elaborate entablature erectly and, in the man's case, even fiercely. Both he and his companion bristle with the symbols of fecundity. Both wear crowns of fruit, and both wear costumes made of trophies and exuviae. Draped around his head, shoulders, and abdomen, much like a priest's garb, are rams' fleeces, and rams' skulls form shoulderpieces. Vincenzo Cartari (1556) tells us that sacrificed rams signify God as the author and maintainer of life.[18] Such "maintainers" are particularly suitable, of course, in this architectural role. And the term grows out of an altar adorned with lions' heads (symbols of the sun and its powers, and of magnanimity[19]), and with fruits and flowers. An oval shield, partly framed with flowers, partly with an astragal necklace, displays a figure of Fame, a divinity with two trumpets who runs barefoot across the earth, her peplos girded up[20] with a medallion marked with an S—for Sapientia, perhaps, suggesting good as opposed to bad fame. The shield is crowned by the image's pendant penis and testicles: the sources of his fruitfulness and valor, no doubt. (The ancients believed that the soul resided both in the head and in the genitals.[21] In antiquity most terms consisted of upright stone markers carved with these two organs only.)

The imagery of Sambin's tenth term portrays the "terminology" we have discussed. At the base of the pedestal the metaphorical draperies turn into true shaft flutes, but the shaft itself stands on a trio of claws clutching the altar's base. One thinks of the moldings on the Erechtheum that were called ὄνυχες, talons. The term's βάσις, foot, is a true foot, with claws; the flutes are ῥάβδοι, pipes, but the other objective correlative for flutes, Vitruvius's drapery folds, are also present. The astragal is a true necklace; the garlands of leaves, fruit, and volutes hang in naturalistic profusion rather then being forced into the abstract shapes of architectural ornament. And, on the priest's head, an echinus of leaves and fruit, suitably shaggy in profile, acts as a cushion for the entablature.

As in the Medici Chapel, this entablature forms an abstract foil for the naturalistic part of the design. It consists of fluted fascia, astragal, palmettes, waterleaf cyma, and so on, of the most normal

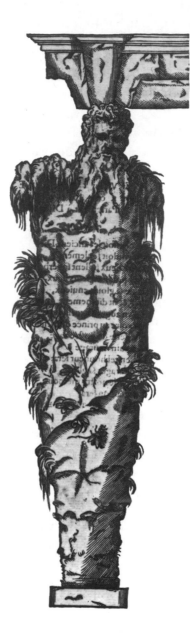

72
Hugues Sambin, First male
term. From *De la Diversité
des Termes*, 1572.

73
Hugues Sambin, First
female term. From *De la
Diversité des Termes,* 1572.

74
Hugues Sambin, Seventh
male term. From *De la
Diversité des Termes*, 1572.

75
Hugues Sambin, Seventh
female term. From *De la
Diversité des Termes*, 1572.

76
Hugues Sambin, Tenth
male term. From *De la
Diversité des Termes*, 1572.

77
Hugues Sambin, Tenth
female term. From *De la
Diversite des Termes,* 1572.

78
Hugues Sambin,
Eighteenth male term.
From *De la Diversité des
Termes*, 1572.

79
Hugues Sambin,
Eighteenth female term.
From *De la Diversité des
Termes*, 1572.

type. The upper corona is a claw molding without eggs, responding to the naturalistic claws of the base. The oval shield inscribed with Fame thus hangs on a sort of trophy in which all the tropes of column terminology are arrayed.

The woman (figure 77), coiffed not only with fruit but with a veil, is dressed in a sort of cuirass consisting of a lyre-shaped stomacher with lions' heads for the shoulders. Between her breasts is a horn-hatted skull. The stomacher contains the scene of a trophy; a captured nude prisoner is attached to a stake and a shield hangs above. The existence of this trophy reinforces my interpretation of the whole term *as* a trophy. On it a winged female figure in a peplos has inscribed a reversed S—perhaps a reference to the bad Sapientia Fame may also circulate. In this case the prisoner could portray the reward of ill fame. The term rises from a pedestal or altar dressed with rams' fleeces, while a ram's skull takes its place at her groin. A garland of fruit and flowers is cross-girded below this, and a set of upright acanthus leaves forms the lowest part of the shaft. The whole complex has a triple-claw base similar to that supporting the male term.

Finally we come to the eighteenth and last pair of terms (figures 78, 79), which belong to the Supercomposite order. With them, gender diagnosis is difficult. Both priest and priestess preside over altars on which stand images of the three Graces, their arms around each others' shoulders.[22] The mainly female term has a torso consisting of a similar group, but her legs are encased in an altar topped with a frieze of rams' heads with interlocked horns. Above the altar proper is a layer of breasts just beneath the Graces. This term, the female Supercomposite, has three faces, like an allegory of Prudence, or of Past, Present, and Future. She supports a curious Doric entablature with Egyptian metopes. Perhaps the two, with their images of sacrifice, fruitfulness, and magnanimity (I refer respectively to the skulls, the breasts and fruit, and the eagles) brought together under a lion-faced aegis supported by genii, is intended to signify complete sufficiency or productiveness. This is a proper theme for the last, summarizing, couple in Sambin's series. The whole of the sacrifice is dedicated to the goddesses of beauty, just as in more normal facades the Corinthian order, representing young girls, is to decorate the upper story.[23] With Hugues Sambin, the tradition of the orders as sacrifical images is lavishly fulfilled.

Conclusion

For an inhabitant of the Hellenistic world, the words "Doric," "echinus," or "Ionic fascia," in Greek, did not have the purely workaday associations they have for us. They suggested bound and decorated victims, ribboned exuviae set on high, gods, cults, ancestors, colonies. Temples were read as concretions of sacrificial matter, of the things that were put into graves and laid on walls and stelai. This sense of architectural ornament is very different from the urge to beauty. But indeed the word ornament, in origin, has little to do with beauty. It means something or someone that has been equipped or prepared, like a hunter, soldier, or priest. Aeneas prepares his father's funeral: *Aeneas patris ornavit exsequias* (Hyginus, *Fabulae*, 173.14). The word has implications of honor, achievement, religious duty. An ornamented temple is one prepared to honor the god. In the Renaissance this vision was revived and developed. We looked at the contributions of Francesco di Giorgio, Michelangelo, Raphael, and some of the treatise writers. Many others could have been studied.

But today this sense of ornament's meaning has once again been lost; for centuries we have been the heirs of a scientific philology that drains architecture of its poetry. Rationalistic etiologies have been the order of the day. Vitruvius's tale about the origins of *building* in the construction of huts from tree trunks and wattles is still examined; but his myths about the origins of *architecture*, about Dorus, Ion, the Corinthian girl, the women of Caryae and the Persian warriors, have seldom been taken seriously by architectural historians. The Vitruvius edition published by Guillaume Philandrier in 1550, which has an index of Greek words and which comments briefly on each one, marked a step toward this austerer scholarship. The austerity was amplified in 1566 and 1567 when

Daniele Barbaro published Italian and Latin editions of an annotated Vitruvius. Barbaro's edition, which contains the most detailed commentary ever composed on Vitruvius's text, abandoned the aspects of Vitruvius's thought that had entranced Francesco di Giorgio and Cesare Cesariano. And the fables we have speculated about get the shortest possible shrift.[1]

Nonetheless there are post-Renaissance examples of what I have discussed. Philology has not staged a clean sweep. The centuries after Sambin have had their Doric columns as Dorian warriors, their caryatids, Persian prisoners, and the like. So I cannot resist one final, "modern" example: the design in the Bibliothèque Nationale by J.-J. Lequeu for what he calls the "symbolic order" for a Hall of States (figure 80).[2] On the right we see the austere masonry wall of a Neoclassical temple. The lower part of the design consists of a denticulated cornice, so we are probably looking at the atlante or herm for an upper floor. A fluted shaft rises from an exiguous Ionic base to form an altar-pedestal from whose top, which is an urn, there emerges the large, round-shouldered torso of a captured aristocrat. His face frowns with effort and humiliation. His lace neckcloth dangles down to his sash, which is that of the Bourbon Order of the Holy Spirit. He wears a cape—and chains. From his head rises a flowery capital that terminates in feminine volutes, possibly a reference to the enormous wigs of *ancien régime* courtiers. The frieze in the upper cornice is decorated, according to the inscription, with "demons with fleurons, interlaced with scrolls of foliage, fitted out with rifles, pistols, and swords, pursuing the monster of enormous grandeur and dreadful shape that appeared July 12 near the Sovereign's palace. This hideous beast with a thousand human heads, vomiting fire and flames mixed with black smoke, seemed to feed on the blood of the French people."

The monster with a thousand heads, we learn—the beast sacrificed, the enemy overthrown—is the civil guard that fired on a crowd near the Louvre two days before the storming of the Bastille. Lequeu's prisoner, then, as is proper, supports a frieze made of the weapons of captured enemies. It is a frieze of exuviae. Helping to support the palace of the people, he admonishes future

80
J.-J. Lequeu, Order for the
Hall of States, 1789.
Bibliothèque Nationale,
Paris.

generations exactly like the Persian and caryatid porticoes in Vitruvius. As a herm he marks the boundary of the new age. As a term he embodies untransgressable boundaries, justice done and seen to be done. He is a Parisian Persian in the New Sparta of revolutionary France.

But Lequeu's careful adaptation of traditional Greco-Roman and Renaissance meanings is not typical of his age. Instead, then and since, we have had not only philology but formalism: the repetition and variation of forms for their own sake, irrespective of their literary, associational, and poetic meanings, and irrespective also of their mythical origins. Yet even in a purely formal world new architectural meanings can be generated. At the end of chapter 2 I likened the classical formulas for symmetry, scale, and proportion to taboos. Even earlier I said that unless we understand these taboos we cannot understand what happens when they are broken. We can put this another way: when that breaking is understood, meanings develop.

Robert Venturi, in a recent unbuilt project for a house based on Mount Vernon, George Washington's residence near Washington D. C., provides a case in point. Prominently featured on Mount Vernon's northern end is an elegant ground-floor Palladian window (figure 81).[3] Without knowing anything about the window's designer, one suspects that he was working from the woodcuts in an English architectural pattern book. The detail has some of the bulky simplification one sees in such images. The low placement of the window is perhaps something of a solecism, as is its richness in comparison to the exceedingly sparse detailing of its surrounding wall. Otherwise it is literate; it does not particularly break the taboos of the English late baroque.

Now let us look at what Venturi does with Washington's window, and with its setting (figures 82, 83). Mount Vernon has been criticized, rightly, for being a pastiche of disparate elements. Examples are the over-attenuated piers that support the famous portico and the extremely irregular fenestration. A third example is this inappropriately rich window. Anyone versed in the canon, the taboos, of classicism would mention these failures. Another architect,

81
Fairfax County, Virginia,
Mount Vernon, Palladian
window, 1776 and after.

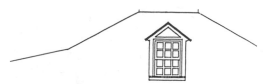

82
Robert Venturi, Palladian
window from project for a
country house, 1979.

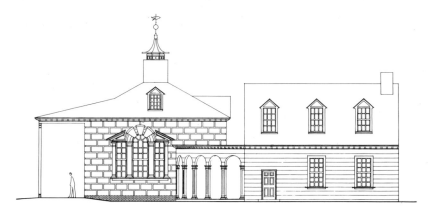

SIDE ELEVATION

83
Robert Venturi, Project for
a country house, 1979.

versed in these matters and recreating Mount Vernon, would probably normalize them—thicken the portico supports, realign the windows on a regular grid, and distribute enrichments more uniformly.[4]

Venturi, however, has not tried to smooth over these expressions of provincial misprision. He has seized on them. He exaggerates them. Perhaps he thought that, since to British eyes Washington was the greatest of profaners, Mount Vernon's architectural profanations should be consecrated into a new orthodoxy. In any event Venturi's portico piers are even thinner than the originals, quite impossibly thin; his fenestration is *more* irregular. Above all he has made the elegant Palladian window massive, almost barbaric. Its huge wedge-shaped voussoirs splay apart the delicate broken pediment and force themselves ferociously inward. The blocky moldings of the original are even blockier. And where the Mount Vernon window is more or less on the axis of the house's ridgepole, chimneys, and dormers, as it should be, in Venturi it is set jarringly off center.

Yet, speaking of broken taboos, to joke thus about Mount Vernon is a sort of blasphemy. To most Americans Mount Vernon is one of childhood's sacred legends. For at least 150 years, judging by the shelves of books and pamphlets on Washington's home that began to be published in the early nineteenth century, the house has been quite literally worshiped. I need not cite chapter and verse on this familiar hagiography. Still today the house is a temple, administered by a self-perpetuating race of priestesses, the Mount Vernon Ladies' Association. In essence, these women conduct pilgrimages and retreats. They keep the shrine sacred. I shall not try to equate Mount Vernon with the temples at Paestum, let alone that at Paphos, nor suggest that its parsimonious dentils and exiguous coronas express the battles, sacrifices, and victories of its most famous resident. But the parallels are not out of line.

Against this background let us take another look at what Venturi has done. Like the composer Charles Ives, he has turned provincial solecisms into savage virtues. But in doing so he has inevitably reacted to this other inheritance, the building's sanctity—again like Ives, who loved to parody favorite hymns. Indeed Venturi's ritual malfeasance only works if we recognize it as such. It is not enough simply to know the proportions and distributions of an orthodox Palladian window. We must also know Mount Vernon, an icon, like the Empire State Building or the Brooklyn Bridge, that is so famous that recognition blots out observation. It is only by wilfully misreading *that* portico, *that* Palladian window, that Venturi's meaning, and our understanding, are achieved.

All of which brings us, rather unexpectedly, back to that realm of the holy versus the unholy that has been a major concern of this book. These are some of the ways, even in an age of formalism and philology, we can still hear classical architecture's continuing voices. They are the voices of history as well as the present. A modernist converses only with his contemporaries and immediate predecessors. But an architect who takes on a Palladian window converses with Palladio, and (in Venturi's case) with Serlio, Hawksmore, Lutyens. He stands in a succession that goes back to the Renaissance and perhaps further still to the mythical dawn pictured by Vitruvius and his contemporaries.

Notes

1

Troping Ornament

1

A. W. N. Pugin, *The True Principles of Pointed or Christian Architecture*, London, 1841, 54.

2

For recent scholarship on Vitruvius, see Silvio Ferri, *Vitruvio, Architettura dai libri i–vii*, Rome, 1960; P. Gros, "Vitruve: l'architecture et sa théorie des études récentes," *Aufstieg und Niedergang der römischen Welt*, 2, 30, 1, 1982, 659ff.; A. Birnbaum, "Vitruvius und die griechische Architektur," *Denkschrift des akademie der Wissenschaften*, Vienna, 1914; Axel Boìthius, "Vitruvius and the Roman Architecture of his Age," Δράγμα *M. P. Nilsson dedicatum*, Acta institutae Romanae Regni Sueciae, 2, 1, Lund, 1939, 114ff. Fuller bibliographies are in L. Callebat, P. Bouet, Ph. Fleury, M. Zuinghedau, *Vitruve. De Architectura. Concordance*, Hildesheim, 1984, *1*, viiff.; and Heiner Knell, *Vitruvs Architekturtheorie*, Hildesheim, 1985, 175ff.

3

L. Callebat, "La Prose du 'De Architectura' de Vitruve," *Aufstieg und Niedergang der römischen Welt*, 2, 30, 1, 1982, 696ff.

4

Designer of the Temple of Dionysus at Teos and that of Artemis Leukophryene at Magnesia. For more on Hermogenes, see Vitruvius 7, Pref. 12; D. S. Robertson, *A Handbook of Greek and Roman Architecture*, Cambridge, 1929, 153ff; H. Knell, "Der Hermogenes-Anekdote und das Ende des dorischen Ringhallentempels," in *Vitruv-Kolloquium des Darmstadtsche Archäologische Verein, Darmstadt, 1982*, 1984; P. Gros, "Le Dossier vitruvien d'Hermogénès," *Mélanges d'archéologie et d'histoire de l'école française de Rome*, 90, 1978, 687ff. For more on Vitruvius's Greek background, see E. Pernice and W. H. Gross, "Die griechischen und lateinischen literarischen Zeugnisse," in U. Hausmann et al., eds., *Handbuch der Archäologie, 1*, Munich, 1969, 410ff.; and B. Wesenberg, "Zu den Schriften griechischer Architekten," in *Bauplanung und Bautheorie der Antike. Kolloquium Architektur-Referat des Deutscher Archäologisches Instituts, 4*, Berlin, 1984, 39ff.

5

Cratylus, 406b. Plato may here be speaking ironically, given the meanings and implications of the word "Artemis" discussed in chapter 3.

6

Quintilian, *Institutiones,* 9.1.5.

7

Sigmund Freud, *Totem and Taboo* [1913], New York, 1950, 5.

8

J. J. Rousseau, *Essai sur l'origine des langues* [1783], III.

9

Giambattista Vico, *La Scienza nuova seconda* [1744], Naples, 1953, paras. 615, 659, 694.

10

The echinus plant is defined by Liddell and Scott, *A Greek-English Lexicon,* ed. Sir H. S. Jones, Oxford, 1968, s.v., as being similar to basil, but it could also be the *echinops* or ball thistle, which has delicately spiky blue blossoms similar in shape to the sea urchin. Hellmut Baumann, *Die griechische Pflanzenwelt in Mythos, Kunst, und Literatur,* Munich, 1982, fig. 424.

11

Klaus Herrmann, "Zum Dekor dorischer Kapitelle," *Architectura, 13,* 1, 1983, 1ff.

2

Architecture and Sacrifice

1

Carl Boetticher, *Der Baumkultus der Hellenen,* Berlin, 1856, 9.

2

Pliny, *Historia naturalis,* 12.1, 12.2. See also Phaedrus, *Fabulae,* 3.17.

3

Bogdan Rutkowski, *The Cult Places of the Aegean,* New Haven, 1986, 101. For more on sacred trees, 107ff.

4

Lucian, *Erotes,* 6.15.

5

Stephanus Byzantinus, s.v. "Pelops."

6

Lucian, *Erotes,* 16. G. F. Hill reports that tree worship survived on Cyprus in his own day [1940]: "Trees which are supposed to cure diseases are hung by devotees with rags of clothing or hair from their heads." *A History of Cyprus, 1,* Cambridge, 1940, 63n.

7

Boetticher, *Baumkultus,* 486ff.

8

Aristophanes, Scholiast, 617, quoted by Boetticher, *Baumkultus,* 11.

9

Boetticher, *Baumkultus,* 14.

10

Rutkowski, *Cult Places,* 54ff.

11

Boetticher, *Baumkultus,* 155.

12

A. W. Lawrence, *The Architecture of Ancient Greece,* 3rd ed., New York, 1950, 123ff.; D. S. Robertson, *A Handbook of Greek and Roman Architecture,* Cambridge, 1929, 5.

13

Rutkowski, *Cult Places,* 101.

14

Pausanias, 10.5.9 Jeffrey Hurwit calls my attention to the early laurel temple (Building H) at Eretria, which apparently imitates this supposed original.

15

Apollodorus, *Epitome,* 2.5; Pindar, Olympian Ode 1, 75ff.; Pausanias, 6.21.9–11.

16

Walter Burkert, *Homo necans: The Anthropology of Ancient Greek Sacrificial Ritual and Myth,* Berkeley, 1983, 3ff.

17

Richard Broxton Onians, *The Origins of European Thought about the Body, the Mind, the Soul, the World, Time, and Fate . . .* , Cambridge, 1951, 271ff. See also G. S. Kirk, "Some Methodological Pitfalls in the Study of Ancient Greek Sacrifice," *Entretiens sur l'antiquité classique,* 27. *Le Sacrifice dans l'antiquité,* Fondation Hardt, Geneva, 1980, 64; also Paul Stengel, *Die griechischen Kultusaltertümer,* Munich, 1898, passim, and Marcel Detienne and Jean-Pierre Vernant, *La Cuisine du sacrifice en pays grec,* Paris, 1979, passim and especially chapter 2.

18

Burkert, *Homo necans,* 177ff.

19

Burkert, *Homo necans,* 232.

20

Helene P. Foley, *Ritual Irony. Poetry and Sacrifice in Euripides,* Ithaca, 1985, 46ff. See also A. Schnapp, "Pratiche ed immagini di caccia nella Grecia antica," *Dia-*

loghi di archeologia, n.s. *1,* 1979, 36ff., and J. K. Anderson, *Hunting in the Ancient World,* Berkeley, 1985.

21

Burkert, *Homo necans,* 73ff.

22

Jean-Pierre Vernant, "Théorie générale du sacrifice et mise à mort dans la θυσία grècque," *Entretiens sur l'antiquité classique, 27,* 10; Burkert, *Homo necans,* 138; Stengel, *Kultusaltertümer,* 116.

23

Vernant, "Sacrifice et mise à mort," 17; Erika Simon, *Festivals of Attica,* Madison, Wis., 1983, 9.

24

H. Hubert and M. Mauss, *Sacrifice, its Nature and Function* [1899], Chicago, 1964, 68; Vernant, "Sacrifice et mise à mort," 18.

25

Hubert and Mauss, *Sacrifice,* 32ff. See also James Frazer, *The Golden Bough: Taboo and the Perils of the Soul,* 3rd ed., London, 1911, 186ff.; Friedrich Schwenn, "Die Menschenopfer bei den Griechen und Römern," *Religionsgeschichtliche Versuche und Vorarbeiten, 15,* 1915, esp. 20ff., 71ff., 104ff.; E. O. James, *Sacrifice and Sacrament,* London, 1962, 77ff.; Burkert, *Homo necans,* 76.

26

Strictly speaking, σπλάγχνα are the edibles such as flesh, heart, and liver, though the word also refers to the lungs.

27

Vernant, "Sacrifice et mise à mort," 8.

28

Burkert, *Homo necans,* 52.

29

Burkert, *Greek Religion,* Cambridge, Mass., 1985, 267; *Homo necans,* 47ff.

30

Burkert, *Homo necans,* 66. The true apotheosis of the trophy is not the temple but the Roman triumphal arch. This is an atoning gesture from the triumphator to the foes he has slain and the peoples he has enslaved. He must purify himself from the taboo attached to these deeds before entering the *pomaerium* or sacred walls of the city. Hence the object that memorializes this purification takes the form of a gate. Ferdinand Noack, "Triumph und Triumphbogen," *Vorträge der Bibliothek Warburg, 5,* 1925–26, 147ff., esp. 151ff. For Greek battle-offerings, see Stengel, *Kultusaltertümer,* 81ff., and Burkert, *Greek Religion,* 69ff. In this sense it is appropriate that among other things the word *exuviae* means 1) armor and weapons stripped from battlefield corpses, and 2) the attributes of gods carried in procession. Plautus, *Epidicus,* 38; Suetonius, *Nero,* 6.4. For Greek and Roman trophies, see W. K. Pritchett, *Greek State at War,* Berkeley, 1979, 2, 259. See also Karl Woelcke, "Beiträge zur Geschichte der Tropaions," *Bonner Jarbücher, 120,* 1911, 127ff., esp. 147ff.; A. J. Janson, *Het Antike Tropaion,* Ghent, 1957; Gilbert Charles-Picard, *Les trophées romains,* Paris, 1957.

31
Rutkowski, *Cult Places,* 111ff.

32
Also known as νεϱτεϱία; see W. H. Roscher, *Lexikon der griechischen und römischen Mythologie,* Leipzig, 1884–86, 7, 48.

33
Onians, *Origins,* 95.

34
An arris, strictly speaking the joint between Doric flutes only, is in Latin *arista,* a word of unknown origin that refers to the extrusion or protrusion of points in vegetable or animal forms—e.g., the beard on a barley oat or the pucker in the flesh of a frightened person.

35
For Vitruvius's Greek terms, see P. Ruffel, "Mots grecs dans Vitruve," in *Hommages à J. Bayet,* Brussels, 1964 (Collection Latomus 70), 627ff.

36
Onians, *Origins,* 115, 119. For the importance of heads in ancient religion, see S. Eitrem, *Beiträge zur griechischen Religionsgeschichte. 1. Der vor-dorische Widdergott,* Christiania, 1910, 34ff.

37
Lucy T. Shoe, *The Profiles of the Greek Mouldings,* Cambridge, Mass. 1936, 8.

38
Onians, *Origins,* 105ff.

39
Onians, *Origins,* 236.

40
Veronica Tatton-Brown, *Cyprus BC. 7000 Years of History,* London, British Museum, 1979, no. 254.

41
Vincent Scully, *The Earth, The Temple, and the Gods,* New Haven, 1962, rev. ed. 1979.

42
Eitrem, *Beiträge,* 3.

43
Onians, *Origins,* 182, 98. For the use of thighbones in sacrifice, see Stengel, *Kultusaltertümer,* 18.

44

Burkert, *Homo necans*, 2.

45

Burkert, *Homo necans*, 2. For early triglyphs in archaeology, see Robertson, *Handbook*, 30ff.

46

Allan Marquand, "On the Terms *cyma recta* and *cyma reversa*," *American Journal of Archaeology*, ser. 2, *10*, 1906, 282ff.

47

ἀκύμων, on the other hand, means barren, without offspring; and the verb κυέω refers to being pregnant. So there are tropes of fecundity involved.

48

Stengel, *Kultusaltertümer*, 85.

49

Epistula, ed. Moses Hadas, New York, 1973, 62ff. See also Shoe, *Profiles*, 1ff.

50

Supplementum epigraphicum graecum [second century B.C.], ed. P. Roussel et al., Leyden, 1923ff., 4.448.

51

Burkhardt Wesenberg, "Kymation und Astragal," *Marburger Winckelmann-Programm*, 1972, 12.

52

Kirk, "Pitfalls," 77; Walter Burkert, "Glaube und Verhalten: Zeichengehalt und Wirkungsmacht von Opferritualen," *Entretiens sur l'antiquité classique*, 27, 117.

53

Onians, *Origins*, 112.

54

Wesenberg, "Kymation und Astragal," 1ff.

55

Shoe, *Profiles*, 8.

56

Schnapp, "Pratiche," and Anderson, *Hunting in the Ancient World*, passim.

57

A corruption of "periment," which in turn is a corruption of "pyramid."

58

Onians, *Origins*, 145, 478 n. 2.

59

E. Lapalus, *Le Fronton sculpté en Grèce, des origines à la fin du IVme siècle*, Paris, 1947, 66.

60

The soffit is based on the plate on 142r in Serlio's *Tutte l'opere d'architettura*, Venice, 1619.

61

Robert Garland, *The Greek Way of Death*, Ithaca, 1985, 119.

62

Quoted by Burkert, *Homo necans*, 39.

63

Giulia Piccaluga, "L'Olocausto di Patrai," *Entretiens sur l'antiquité classique*, 27, 243ff.

64

Anthologia palatina, 6.111ff.; Philostratus, *Imagines*, 1.28.

65

Livy, 3.55, 7. See also Stengel, *Kultusaltertümer*, 138ff.; Eduard Williger, "Hagios. Untersuchungen zur Terminologie des Heiligen in den Hellenisch-Hellenistischen Religionen," *Religionsgeschichtliche Versuche und Vorarbeiten, 19*, 1922; Mary Douglas, *Purity and Danger*, London, 1966; Louis Gernet, *Anthropologie de la Grèce antique*, Paris, 1968; Louis Moulinier, *Le Pur et l'impur dans la pensée des grecs, d'Homère à Aristote. Etudes et commentaires, 11*, Paris, 1952, 117; Jean-Pierre Vernant, *Mythe et pensée chez les Grecs*, Paris, 1965; Garland, *Greek Way of Death*, 46; Burkert, *Greek Religion*, 64ff., 80ff., 269ff.

66

Which is why when René Girard's admirable book *Le Violence et le sacré* was translated as *Violence and the Sacred*, the title changed meaning.

67

Frazer, *The Golden Bough*, 2, 7ff.; Herodotus, 1.99. Dario Sabbatucci, "Sacer," *Studi e materiali di storia delle religioni*, 24–25, 1952, 92ff.

68

Georg Hock, "Griechische Weihegebräuche," diss., Munich, 1905, 73ff. and 77ff., describes the consecration of temple foundation stones. These are sprinkled, blessed, anointed, etc., just like living sacrifices. See also Martin P. Nilsson, *Geschichte der griechischen Religion, 1*, Munich, 1941, 379 n. 1; for building sacrifices outside Greece, see K. Klusemann, *Das Bauopfer*, Graz-Hamburg, 1919.

69

Burkert, *Homo necans*, 49. See also Jean Casabona, *Recherches sur le vocabulaire des sacrifices en grec, des origines à la fin de l'époque classique*, Aix-en-Provence, 1966.

3

Images of Temple Founders

1

See E. A. Gardner, D. G. Hogarth, M. R. James, and R. E. Smith, "Excavations on Cyprus, 1887–1888," *Journal of the Hellenic Society*, 9, 1888, 270, and Max Ohnefalsch-Richter, *Kypros, die Bibel und Homer*, 1, Berlin, 1893, 23ff. For the current campaigns at Paphos, see F. G. Maier, "Temple of Aphrodite at Kouklia (Old Paphos)," *Report of the Department of Antiquities*, [Republic of Cyprus] (hereafter *RDAC*), 1965–67, 86ff., and almost every year since, esp. Maier, "The Temple of Aphrodite at Old Paphos," *RDAC*, 1975, 67ff. See also the same author's *Brief History and Description of Old Paphos (Kuklia)*, Nicosia, n.d., and his "The Paphian Shrine of Aphrodite and Crete," *International Archaeological Symposium "The Relations between Cyprus and Crete, ca. 2000–500 BC"*, Nicosia, 1978, 228ff. For Paphos's sacred grove, see Wilhelm H. Engel, *Kypros, eine Monographie*, 1, Berlin, 1841, 203ff.

2

Hesiod, *Theogony*, 188ff.

3

RDAC, 1976, 93.

4

Clement of Alexandria, *Protrepticon*, 2.13.2; Arnobius, *Contra nationes*, 5.19. For a very full discussion, see s.v. "Phallos," *Paulys' Real-Enzyklopädie der classichen Altertumswissenschaft*, 1696ff., 1710ff. Also Walter Burkert, *Homo necans: The Anthropology of Ancient Greek Sacrificial Ritual and Myth*, Berkeley, 1983, 82ff.

5

Alfred Westholm, "The Paphian Temple of Aphrodite and its Relation to Oriental Architecture," *Acta archaeologica* [Copenhagen], 4, 1933, 217. G. F. Hill, *A History of Cyprus*, 1, Cambridge, 1940, 75n. Cf. also the older literature, A. F. Gori [and G. B. Passeri], *Thesaurus gemmarum antiquarum astriferarum . . .* , Florence, 1750, pls. 77, 78; pp. lxxviii and 118; also Ennius Quirinus Visconti, *Musée Pie-Clémentin*, 1, Milan, 1818, 351, pl. A.IX, no. 19; also C. G. Lenz, *Die Göttin von Paphos auf alten Bildwerken und Baphomet*, Gotha, 1808; D. Friedrich Münter, *Der Tempel der himmlischen Göttin zu Paphos*, Copenhagen, 1824; H. de Luynes, *Numismatique et inscriptions cypriotes*, Paris, 1852; T. L. Donaldson, *Architectura numismatica*, London, 1859, 107ff.; Gardner, Hogarth, James, et al., "Excavations on Cyprus," 210ff.; G. F. Hill, *A Catalogue of the Greek Coins of Cyprus*, London, 1904, lxiiff., pls. xiv–xvii, and xxvi; Christian Blinkenberg, *Le Temple de Paphos* [Det Kgl. Danske Videnskabernes Selskab.] *Historisk—filologiske Meddelelser*, 9.2, Copenhagen, 1924; Maier, "Temple of Aphrodite," *RDAC*, 1975, 71n, and Maier, "Temple of Aphrodite," *RDAC*, 1976, 75ff.

6

Cyprus Museum C. S. 18 (74.51.2464). V. Karageorghis, *The Civilisation of Pre-historic Cyprus*, Athens, c. 1976, 68. See also C. F. A. Schaeffer, *Missions en Chypre, 1932–1935*, Paris, 1936, and Hans-Günter Buchholz and Vassos Karageorghis, *Prehistoric Greece and Cyprus*, London, 1971, 161. Another relative of the Paphos shrine was erected three hundred years after it: Sanctuary I was built in the ninth century B.C. by Phoenicians at nearby Kition and was probably dedicated to Astarte. See V. Karageorghis, *Kition. Mycenaean and Phoenician Discoveries in Cyprus*, London, 1976, 79. See also A. L. Evans, "Mycenaean Tree and Pillar Cult and its Mediterranean Relations," *Journal of Hellenic Studies*, *21*, 1900, 104.

7

From a myth recorded by Nigidius Figulus. W. H. Roscher, *Lexikon der griechischen und römischen Mythologie*, Leipzig, 1884–86, s.v. "Aphrodite," col. 393.

8

Sergio Ribichini, *Adonis*, Rome, 1980, 92ff.

9

Paul Stengel, *Die griechischen Kultusaltertümer*, Munich, 1898, 85.

10

Pindar, Olympian Ode 13, 21 75ff. For the doves, Münter, *Paphos*, 25ff.; Evans, "Mycenaean Tree and Pillar Cult," 105; Max Ohnefalsch-Richter, *Kypros*, *1*, 278ff. and figs. 181, 182, 186; and Engel, *Kypros*, 2, 181. The Paphiote shrine is often likened to the model dove-shrines made of gold and found in tombs at Mycenae. These had been buried with small gold images of naked Aphrodite-like goddesses who had doves perched on their heads and shoulders. Evans, "Mycenaean Tree and Pillar Cult," 104ff., 191ff.

11

J. L. Myres, *Handbook of the Cesnola Collection of Antiquities from Cyprus*, New York, 1914, nos. 1151–52, 1204–22.

12

"Horns of consecration," similar to those found in Mycenaean excavations, some large and of limestone, have been found at Paphos. Maier, "The Temple of Aphrodite," *RDAC*, 1976, 95; Maier, "Excavation at Kuklia (Palaepaphos), 1973," *RDAC*, 1974, 137. For horns on temple facades in general, see Martin Nilsson, *Geschichte der griechischen Religion*, Munich, 1955–61, *1*, 251ff.; for Cyprus, M. C. Loulloupis, "Mycenaean Horns of Consecration in Cyprus," *Acts of the International Archaeological Symposium*, "The Relations between Cyprus and Crete, ca. 2000–500 BC," Nicosia, 1979, 102–103.

13

Lucian, *De Dea Syria*, 16, 28, 29; see also Arnobius, *Adversus gentes*, 5.19; Nilsson, *Geschichte*, *1*, 494.

14

Burkert, *Homo necans*, 83; Walter Burkert, *Greek Religion*, Cambridge, Mass., 1985, 257, 292.

15

A. F. Gori, *Thesaurus gemmarum antiquarum astriferarum*, Florence, 1750, pls. 77, 78.

16

Aside from the columns and bird-formed "tympanum," the facade proper consists of a lower housing for the baetyl and, at least in coins of Vespasian and Titus, a double beam or simplified entablature. See Hill, *Catalogue*, pl. xv. In some coins, and in Donaldson's reconstruction (figure 24), the arrangement suggests an upper floor with three windows. We can also read it as an entablature.

17

However, the two central horned columns do not support an entablature but act as pylons between which the entablature is set. Engel, *Kypros*, 2, 192; Max Ohnefalsch-Richter, *Kypros*, *1*, 133; Evans, "Mycenaean Tree and Pillar Cult," 118.

18

Blinkenberg, *Temple de Paphos*, 10. Roscher, *Lexikon*, s.v. "Astarte," cols. 651–53. Vassos Karageorghis and Jean des Gagniers, describing an Ion Age krater of the Bichrome III type now in the Cyprus Museum, Nicosia (B1988), conclude that the artist decorated the pot with two views of the Paphiote temple in actual use. They see worshipers or priests standing before and within the building. The one or more human heads that appear at roof level, the authors continue, probably belong to sacred prostitutes. *La Céramique Chypriote de style figuré. Age du Fer (1050–500 av.J.-C)*, *1*, Rome 1974, 8off. We have already seen how common it was to set women's heads on rooftops (figure 17).

19

The phrase ἱερὸς γάμος seems to have had several meanings. Plato (*Laws*, 841d) uses it to mean "lawful wedlock," though he considers such wedlock possible between a man and several women living together. See also Menander, *Fragmenta*, ed. Kock, 320; Hesychius, ed. Schmidt, 468.56; Anaxandrides Comicus, ed. Kock, 34.2; Pindar, Olympian Ode 13. *Der Kleine Pauly*, Stuttgart, 1972ff., has a list of illustrations of hieroi gamoi in art. See also *Paulys' Real-Enzyklopädie*, Suppl. 6, col. 107; A. Klinz, ΊΕΡΟΣ ΓΑΜΟΣ, Halle, 1933; H. Hexter, "Hetairai," *Reallexikon für Antike und Christentum, 3*, 1957, 1154ff.; H. Hexter, "Des Soziologie der antike Prostitution im Lichte des heidnischen und christliche Schrifttums," *Jahrbuch für Antike und Christentums, 3*, 1960, 7off., *Paulys' Real-Enzyklopädie*, s.v. "Hetairai", col. 1333ff., and Erika Simon, *Opfernde Götter*, Berlin, 1953, 6off.

20

And she could be the model for Aphrodite's temple image. Anatol Semenov, "Hypereides und Phryne," *Klio, 28*, 1935, 271ff.; see also Philostratus, *Apollonius of Tyana,* 6.40; Stengel, *Kultusaltertümer,* 84; Burkert, *Greek Religion,* 239ff.; Burkert, *Homo necans,* 160 nn. 116, 117; 230ff.

21

Vitruvius 4.1.3. See also Herodotus, 1.56. Some of the ideas in this chapter appeared, in preliminary form, in my "The Classical Orders of Architecture as Totems in Vitruvian Myth," *Umanesimo a Roma nel quattrocento,* Rome/New York, 1984, 213ff.

22

See also Friedrich Schwenn, "Der Krieg in der griechischen Religion," *Archiv für Religionswissenschaft, 21,* 1922; E. Bickermann, "Alexandre le Grand et les villes d'Asie," *Revue des études grecques, 47,* 1934, 346ff., esp. 358, 367; and W. K. Pritchett, *The Greek State at War,* Berkeley, 1979.

23

Iliad, 22.63ff., trans. E. V. Rieu, Harmondsworth, 1950, 398. By "Achaean" Homer means Greek.

24

Richard Broxton Onians, *The Origins of European Thought about the Body, the Mind, the Soul, the World, Time, and Fate . . .* , Cambridge, 1951, 4.

25

Cf. Jeffrey M. Hurwit, *The Art and Culture of Early Greece, 1100–480 BC,* Ithaca, 1985, 188, for this and 160 for the quotation from Tyrtaios.

26

A. W. Lawrence, *Greek Architecture,* 4th ed., Harmondsworth, 1983, 116; Hellmut Berve, Gottfried Gruben, and Max Hirmer, *Greek Temples, Theaters and Shrines,* New York, n.d., 346ff. For a more general discussion of the origins of Doric, see Hurwit, *Art and Culture,* 179ff.

27

At Mycale there was a Pan-Ionium temple dedicated to Apollo; Herodotus, 1.148. For Apollo and Artemis Πανιώνια, "all-Ionian," see Roscher, *Lexikon,* s.v. "Panionios," col. 1535. For legends of the Carian colony founders, see S. Eitram, *Beitrage zur griechischen Religionsgeschichte. 1. Der vor-dorische Widdergott,* Christiania, 1910, 165ff.

28

For Ion see Herodotus, 7.94, 9.44; Apollodorus, *The Library,* 1.7.3; Stephanus Byzantinus, s.v. Ἰωνία., and Euripides, *Ion;* also Eitrem, *Beiträge,* 179.

29

Roscher, *Lexikon,* s.v. "Artemis," 568, 574.

30

Lawrence, *Greek Architecture*, 123ff.

31

See also Apollodorus, *The Library*, 1.7.4, 1.7.6.

32

Hippocrates, *Epidemiae*, 3.1; *Aëre*, 4.

33

Gottfried Gruben;, *Die Tempel der Griechen*, Munich, 1986, 241ff.; Angela Pontrandolfo, "Paestum and its Archaeological History," in *Paestum and the Doric Revival, 1750–1830*, National Academy of Design, New York, 1986, 51ff. It was long thought that Paestum was indeed a Doric colony; see Alessio Symmacco Mazzocchi, *Commentariorum en regii herculanensis musei aeneas tabulas heraclenses* . . . , Naples, 1745, 499.

34

E. Lapalus, *Le Fronton sculpté en Grèce, des origines à la fin du IVme siècle*, Paris, 1947; A. Delivorrias, *Attische Giebelskulpturen und Akrotere des fünften Jahrhunderts (Tübingen Studien zur Archäologie und Kunstgeschichte, 1)*, Tübingen, 1974. Ionic temples seem to have had less violent sculptural subject matter than Doric. In addition to the centauromachies and other battles characteristic of Doric temples, there are races, banquets, processions, assemblies of gods, and the like. (But the Doric temple at Corfu had a banquet.) R. Demangel, *La Frise ionique*, Paris, 1932. See also R. Carpenter, "Vitruvius and the Ionic Order," *American Journal of Archaeology, 30*, 1926, 259ff.

35

Lapalus, *Fronton sculpté*, 458ff.

36

Roscher, *Lexikon*, "Artemis," col. 582ff. and "Apollon," col. 440ff.

37

Lawrence, *Greek Architecture*, 161ff.

38

Lucian, *On Sacrifices*, 13; Adolf Claus, "De Dianae antiquissima apud Graecos natura," diss., Breslau, 1881, 36ff.; Schwenn, "Der Krieg," 62ff., Burkert, *Greek Religion*, 151ff.; Claude Calame, *Les Choeurs des jeunes filles en Grèce archaïque*, Rome, 1977, 264ff.

39

See Auguste Schott, "Akanthus," *Jahreshefte des Oesterreichischen Archäologischen Instituts, 44*, 1959, 54ff., esp. 72ff., where he illustrates a lekythos on which are painted pillar tombs crowned with acanthus leaves and women bringing baskets. See also Arthur Fairbanks, *Athenian Lekythoi*, New York, 1907, 172, 309; 1914 ed. pls. 27.2, 29, 31.2, 31.3. I owe these references to J. J. Pollitt. Two short pieces by Joseph Rykwert are also relevant here. "The Corinthian Order," in his *The Necessity of Artifice*, Cambridge, 1980, 33ff.; and "On an (Egyptian?) Misreading of Francesco di Giorgio's," *Res*, 1, Spring 1981, 78ff.

40

For the acanthus plant, or bear's-foot as it is called, see Schott, "Akanthus," and Hellmut Baumann, *Die Griechische Pflanzenwelt in Mythos, Kunst und Literatur*, Munich, 1982 169ff. Baumann points out that the *acanthus mollis*, the plant in question, is not now native to Corinth. For toys and prized possessions in tombs, see Robert Garland, *The Greek Way of Death*, Ithaca, 1985, 84.

41

Carl Boetticher, *Der Baumkultus der Hellenen*, Berlin, 1856, 280, 286ff.

42

Garland, *Greek Way of Death*, 108. Or she could be likened to the loutrophoros, the woman who places a waterjug (for the bridal bath) on the tomb of a girl who dies before marriage; Burkert, *Homo necans*, 221.

43

Onians, *Origins*, 277.

44

Pliny, *Historia naturalis*, 35.92: Pausanias, 1.26.7. Cf. Rykwert, "On a Misreading," 78, and J. J. Pollitt, *The Ancient View of Greek Art*, New Haven, 1974, 194ff., 364ff.

45

Charles Chipiez, *Histoire critique des ordres grecs*, Paris, 1876, 310ff.

46

Der Kleine Pauly, s.v.

47

Ion of Chos, *Tragicorum fragmenta graecorum*, ed. August Nauck, 2nd ed., Leipzig, 1926, frag. 38.

48

To the Greeks (and Romans) baskets had more significance than they do to us. We have seen their lethal role in animal sacrifices. The girls who performed in the Athenian festival of the Arrhephoria, marking the new year, also carried baskets on their heads containing secret things. Burkert, *Greek Religion*, 228ff.

49

Vitruvius does not discuss the Composite order (Corinthian capital with Ionic volutes). The Tuscan temple he describes has columns with very simple capitals, and he does not provide a myth of its origins (4.7).

4

The Caryatid and Persian Porticoes

1

Vitruvius may have been conflating the Persian Wars of the fifth century B.C. with a Spartan expedition against Caryae of 367 B.C. This was part of a civil war in which certain Laconian towns had rebelled against Spartan leadership. Caryae was a rallying point in this revolt (Xenophon, *Historia Hellenica*, 6.5.25, 27). My colleague J. J. Pollitt reminds me that Vitruvius's assumption, namely the possibility of Persian sympathizers in Laconia in 480 B.C., is unlikely. But see Heiner Knell, *Vitruvs Archtekturtheorie*, Darmstadt, 1985, 25. Later, in 370–69 B.C., Caryae was punitively destroyed by Spartans (Xenophon, *Hellenica*, 7.1.28). For the caryatids, see also B. Wesenberg, "Kaiserforum und Akropolis," *Jahrbuch des deutschen archäologischen Instituts, 99*, 1984, 172ff.; H. Plommer, "Vitruvius and the Origin of Caryatids," *Journal of the Hellenic Society, 99*, 1979, 97ff.; H. Drerup, "Zur Bezeichnung 'Karyatide,'" *Marburger Winckelmanns Programm*, 1975–76, 11ff.; and Th. Homolle, "L'Origine des caryatides," *Revue archéologique, 5*, 1917, 1ff. For the etymology of the word, see R. Dant, *Imago*, 1976, 102ff., and C. A. Böttiger, *Amalthea, 3*, 1825, 137ff.

2

Pierre Ducrey, *Le Traitement des prisonniers de guerre dans la Grèce antique*, Paris, 1968, 211. For an interesting new translation of Vitruvius 1.1.5, see Burkhardt Wesenberg, "Die Kopien der Erechtheionkoren und die Frauen von Karyai," *Jahrbuch des deutschen archäologischen Instituts, 99*, 1984, 174.

3

Ducrey, *Prisonniers*, 211, pl. 2; 242.

4

Evamaria Schmidt, *Geschichte der Karyatide*, Würzburg, 1982, 29. For ancient *Stützfiguren* in general, see Schmidt plus Andreas Schmidt-Colinet, *Antike Stützfiguren. Untersuchungen zu Typus und Bedeutung der menschengestaltigen Architekturstütze in der griechischen und römischen Kunst*, Frankfurt-am-Main, 1977, which contains a catalogue. For caryatids and the nut tree see R. Merkelbach, "Gefesselte Götter," *Antaios, 13*, 1971, 549ff.; Martin P. Nilsson, *Geschichte der griechischen Religion, 1*, 1941, 457ff.; and K. A. Rhomaios, ΚΑΡΥΑΤΙΔΕΣ, Πελοποννησιακά, 3–4, 1958–59, 376ff.

5

Pratinas Lyricus, *Fragmenta lyrica*, ed. T. Bergk, 4. Pratinas wrote a tragedy, now lost, called *Caryatides*. See also Claude Calame, *Les Choeurs des jeunes filles en Grèce archaique*, Rome, 1977, 264ff., and Sam Wide, *Lakonische Kulte*, Leipzig, 1893, 102ff. Pliny, *Historia naturalis*, 35.92, says Callimachus, inventor of the

Corinthian capital, executed sculptures of dancing Laconian women. These might have been caryatis dancers.

6

Walter Burkert, *Homo necans: The Anthropology of Ancient Greek Sacrificial Ritual and Myth,* Berkeley, 1983, 250ff.

7

Richard Broxton Onians, *The Origins of European Thought about the Body*, Cambridge, 1951, 29, 400ff.

8

Lewis and Short, *Oxford Latin Dictionary,* s.v. "Caria." See also Thucydides, *Pelopennesian War,* 1.4.8.

9

Burkert, *Homo necans,* 226.

10

For the nuts sacred to Artemis as apotropaic marriage symbols, see Servius on Virgil's *Bucolicum,* 8.29. For the nut tree and caryatids, see Schmidt, *Geschichte,* 29, and Rhomaios, ΚΑΡΥΑΤΙΔΕΣ, passim.

11

Calame, *Choeurs,* 270ff.

12

Pausanias, 4.16.9; Calame, *Choeurs,* 267ff.

13

The oldest known Greek statue-columns decorated the Cnidian Treasury at Delphi, which dates from 565 B.C. The Syphnian Treasury at Delphi, 525 B.C. also had statue-columns. The acanthus columns at Delphi in certain respects suggest caryatids. Schmidt-Colinet, *Antike Stützfiguren,* lists seventy female and eighty-six male *Stützfiguren.* All those earlier in date than the Erechtheum come from Delphi, except those on the throne of Apollo at Amyklai of 510–500 B.C. See also Charles Chipiez, *Histoire critique des origines et de la formation des ordres grecs,* Paris, 1876, 173ff. Schmidt, *Geschichte,* 15ff., discusses the difficulty of separating caryatids from other types of support figures such as atlantes, telamones, etc., and records all the classical texts in which these words appear. For the Erechtheum, see J. M. Paton and G. P. Stevens, *The Erechtheum,* Cambridge, Mass., 1927, and D. S. Robertson, *A Handbook of Greek and Roman Architecture,* Cambridge, 1929, 127ff. For the Erechtheum's caryatids, see Schmidt, *Geschichte,* 79ff.; and Gottfried Gruben, *Die Tempel der Griechen,* Munich, 1986, 193ff.

14

Helmut Berve, Gottfried Gruben, Max Hirmer, *Greek Temples, Theaters, and Shrines,* New York, n.d., 386ff.

15

Fiechter, *Paulys' Real-Enzyklopädie*, s.v. The inscription reads: τοὺς λίθους . . . τοὺς ἐπὶ τῶν κορῶν (*Corpus Inscriptionum Graecarum*, 1.2, 372.86).

16

Burkert, *Greek Religion*, Cambridge, Mass., 1985, 45ff., points out that the Erechtheum is a rare example of a temple erected to replace a megaron or house. See also Burkert, *Homo necans*, 66.

17

Michaelis Apostolius, *Paroemiae*, 15.84. I quote from the edition of Leiden, 1619, 191. But other writers give different numbers. See Roscher, *Lexikon*, s.v., col. 1297.

18

For wartime sister and daughter sacrifice, see Paul Stengel, *Die griechischen Kultusaltertümer*, Munich, 1898, 114ff.

19

One notes that in the Erechtheum Erechtheus received sacrifices at an altar to Poseidon (Pausanias, 1.26.5).

20

Roscher, *Lexikon*, s.v. "Erechtheus," col. 1298.

21

Burkert, *Greek Religion*, 267. Colin Austin, ed., *Nova fragmenta euripidea in papyris reperta*, Berlin, 1968, Frag. 65, Sorbonne Papyrus 2328.

22

Johannes Toeppfer, *Attische Genealogie*, Berlin, 1889, 113ff. and especially 117ff. Also Burkert, *Greek Religion*, 96.

23

Quoted by Burkert, *Homo necans*, 148.

24

In addition, the whole prosperity of Attica proceeds from the conflict between Poseidon and Athena for the rule of Attica. This is the subject of the sculpture on the Parthenon's west pediment.

25

But see Kristian Jeppesen, "Where was the so-called Erechtheion?" *American Journal of Archaeology*, *83*, 1979, 381ff.; and Jeppesen, "Further Inquiries on the Location of the Erechtheion," *American Journal of Archaeology*, *87*, 1983, 325ff. Jeppesen argues that the real Erechtheum was not the present building but a ruined megaron next to it. If the real Erechtheum had no caryatid porch, my argument fails.

26

There was a similar portico, with statues of barbarian captives supporting the roof, at Corinth, whose museum preserves relics of it. See Schmidt, *Geschichte*, 132.

27

W. K. Pritchett, *The Greek State at War*, 2, Berkeley, 1979, 246ff., 259. See also Karl Woelcke, "Beiträge zur Geschichte der Tropaions," *Bonner Jahrbücher, 120*, 1911, 127ff., esp. 147ff.; A. J. Janson, *Het Antike Tropaion*, Ghent, 1957; Gilbert Charles-Picard, *Les trophées romains*, Paris, 1957.

28

Plommer, "Vitruvius," 99ff.

5
Francesco di Giorgio, Michelangelo, and Raphael

1

For Vitruvius in the Renaissance, see the two articles by Lucia A. Ciapponi, "Il 'De Architectura' di Vitruvio nel primo umanesimo," *Italia medioevale e umanistica, 3*, 1960, 59ff., and "Fra Giocondo da Verona and his Edition of Vitruvius," *Journal of the Warburg and Courtauld Institutes, 47*, 1984, especially 72, 82; also Bodo Ebhardt, *Die zehn Bücher der Architektur des Vitruv und ihre Herausgeber (seit 1484)*, [1918] Ossining, NY, 1962. For the orders in the North European Renaissance, see Erik Forssman, *Säule und Ornament*, Uppsala, 1956, and *Dorisch, jonisch, korinthisch: Studien über den Gebrauch der Säulenordnungen in der Architektur des 16.–18 Jahrhunderts*, Stockholm, 1961.

2

Pausanias, 5.1.5ff. However, he mistakenly says they are of bronze and that they are stretching their arms up to the gods rather than supporting the weight of the entablature. But perhaps they do both? The figures could represent the Carthaginian prisoners who constructed temples in Agrigento after the battle of Himera in 480 B.C. (Diodorus Siculus, 11.25.2–5). Cf. D. S. Robertson, *A Handbook of Greek and Roman Architecture*, Cambridge, 1929, 122ff

3

For these see Francesco di Giorgio, *Trattati di architettura, ingegneria e arte militare, 1*, ed. Corrado Maltese, Milan, 1967, xi ff, and Lawrence Lowic, "The Meaning and Significance of the Human Analogy in Francesco di Giorgio's Trattato," *Journal of the Society of Architectural Historians, 62*, 1983, 25ff. n. 1., with the earlier bibliography. For the dating of the treatises, see Richard J. Betts, "On the Chronology of Francesco di Giorgio's Treatises: New Evidence from an Unpublished Manuscript," *Journal of the Society of Architectural Historians, 36*, 1977, 3ff. This discusses manuscript 129 in the Spencer Collection, New York Public Library, which contains interesting variants on the passages discussed below.

4

Francesco di Giorgio, *Trattati*, *1*, 57.

5

Francesco di Giorgio, *Trattati*, *1*, 59ff. See also Joseph Rykwert, "On an (Egyptian?) Misreading of Francesco di Giorgio's," *Res*, *1*, Spring 1981, 78ff.

6

Aristotle, *Historia animalium*, 638 a 31; *Geoponica*, ed. Bergkh, Leipzig, 1895, 5.13.1. Cf. also Lucian, *De Dea Syria*, 58.1, cited above.

7

Yale University, Beinecke Library, MS 491.

8

More specifically, the two statues in the Louvre (figures 44, 45) were carved in 1513–15. The four unfinished ones in the Florence Accademia (figures 46–49) date from the 1520s. But the basic impetus for all these prisoners is recorded in the Florence and Berlin drawings of c. 1513 (figure 50), which in turn record the project of 1505.

9

It is generally agreed that, as the schemes for the tomb developed, the *Captives* came to signify the arts, who became prisoners of Julius's death, since he had been such a great patron. But this explanation came along only after the original planning period of 1503–13, superseding the original meaning. The basic studies for the tomb of Julius II are Erwin Panofsky, "The First Two Projects of Michelangelo's Tomb of Julius I," *Art Bulletin*, *19*, 1937, 561ff., and *Studies in Iconology*, [1939], New York, 1972, 194ff.; Charles de Tolnay, *The Tomb of Julius II*, Princeton, 1954 who notes the influence of the Persian portico *en passant*, p. 27; Howard Hibbard, *Michelangelo*, New York, 1974, 85ff.; 148ff.; and Christoph Luitpold Frommel, "'Capella Iulia': Die Grabkapelle Papst Julius II in Neu-St. Peter," *Zeitschrift für Kunstgeschichte*, *40*, 1977, 26ff. See also Frommel, "Die Peterskirche unter Papst Julius II im Licht neuer Dokumente," *Römisches Jahrbuch für Kunstgeschichte*, *16*, 1976, 57ff.

10

For the herms' uniqueness, see Eugene J. Johnson, "Studies on the Use of Herms in 16th-Century Architecture in Italy," MA thesis, New York University, Institute of Fine Arts, 1963. He discusses Michelangelo's *Captives*, 1ff. For Vitruvius's influence on Michelangelo, see David Summers, *Michelangelo and the Language of Art*, Princeton, 1981, 436, and Bernard Schultz, *Art and Anatomy in Renaissance Italy*, Ann Arbor, 1985, 103ff.

11

Pausanias, 3.3.11.3. The Renaissance translations I have seen render the phrase thus; e.g., Abraham Loescher, trans., *Pausaniae de tote Graecia libri 10*, Basel, 1550, 119: *Ad columnas tum alii Persae ex albo marmore sunt facti*, etc.

12

For possible meanings of the phrase, and bibliography on it, see Evamaria Schmidt, *Geschichte der Karyatide,* Würzburg, 1982, 9.

13

Pierre Ducrey, *Le Traitement des prisonniers de guerre dans la Grèce antique,* Paris, 1968, especially pls. ii (a cup from Sparta in the Vatican on which is painted a nude Prometheus tied to a Doric column), and ix (Roman captives in a relief in Mainz).

14

Ferdinand Noack, "Triumph und Triumphbogen," *Vorträge der Bibliothek Warburg,* 5, pls. vi, vii, viii.

15

See Karl Woelcke, "Beiträge zur Geschichte der Tropaions," *Bonner Jahrbücher, 120,* 1911, pl. xii, no. 52.

16

Among the best known of these were a set of marble reliefs, called caryatids, now in the Palazzo dei Conservatori, Rome. In the Renaissance these were thought to be the statues that Pliny describes as being on the Pantheon, and which *he* called caryatids (*Historia naturalis,* 36.4.38). And indeed, in their supposed original positions, forming a socle for the inner columns of the Hadrianeum, these barbarian provinces would have had a caryatid-like, that is, supportive, role. See W. Helbig, *Führer durch die öffentlicher Sammlungen klassischer Altertümer in Rom,* 2, Tübingen, 1966, no. 1437, with bibliography; also H. Stuart Jones, *A Catalogue of the Ancient Sculptures Preserved in the Municipal Collections of Rome. The Sculptures of the Palazzo dei Conservatori,* Oxford, 1926, 3ff., and C. Jatta, *Le Rappresentazioni figurate delle provincie romane,* Rome, 1908.

17

Panofsky, "First Two Projects," 561ff. Giorgio Vasari, *Vita di Michelangelo,* ed. Paola Barocchi, Milan/Naples, 1962, *1,* 28ff., gives both the 1550 and 1568 texts. Panofsky admits that in the 1505 project the statues were to represent provinces but that in the subsequent versions of the tomb they became souls yearning to remove themselves from their physical bodies so as to attain oneness with God (*Studies,* 194ff). For these and other controversies, see de Tolnay, *Julius II,* passim; Herbert von Einem, *Michelangelo, Bildhauer, Maler, Baumeister,* Berlin, 1973, 45ff., 252 n. 8; and Vasari, *Michelangelo,* ed. Barocchi, *2,* 641ff.

18

Paola Barocchi in Vasari, *Michelangelo, 2,* 293, with bibliography.

19

Pio Paschini, *Roma nel Rinascimento,* Bologna, 1940, 371ff., 388ff. See also Ludwig Pastor, *The History of the Popes, 6,* London, 1898, 216ff., and Francesco

Guicciardini, *La Historia di Italia* [1561] in Guicciardini, *Opere*, ed. V. Caprariis, Milan/Naples, 1953, 629ff.

20

John W. O'Malley, ed., "Fulfillment of the Christian Golden Age under Pope Julius II: Text of a Discourse by Egidio of Viterbo, 1507," *Traditio*, 25, 1969, 265ff., and O'Malley, *Egidio of Viterbo on Church and Reform*, Leiden, 1968. For a later, similar discourse, see Clare O'Reilly, "'Maximus Caesar et Pontifex Maximus': Egidio of Viterbo Proclaims the Alliance between Emperor Maximilian I and Pope Julius II," *Augustiniana*, 22, 1972, 8off. This contains ideas similar to those in the 1507 discourse, though they are less fancifully ambitious.

21

O'Malley, "Discourse," 322, 323, 326. Cf. II Chronicles 36; Ezra 5.2, 6.13ff.; Isaiah 45.

22

Charles L. Stinger, *The Renaissance in Rome*, Bloomington, Ind., 1985, 109 and fig. 8.

23

Even in his last year of life, when mortally ill, Julius saw himself as a liberator. A procession was held in 1513 in which sixteen floats appeared, each devoted to one of his achievements. On the first was a naked woman in chains, her hands tied behind her back: Captive Romagna. In the second was a map of Italia Liberata, showing the provinces and cities Julius or his allies had freed. Other floats represented fettered cities: Bologna, Reggio Emilia, Parma, Piacenza, Genoa, and Savona. Next came Moses with the serpent-staff that erased his enemies and liberated his people, and wagons bearing obelisks inscribed, in several languages, "To Julius II Pontifex Maximus, Liberator of Italy and Extinguisher of Schismatics." Still other floats displayed allegories of Julius's conversion of the peoples of Africa and presented the kings of Europe as crusaders marching under the Pope's command (Paschini, *Roma*, 402ff.). See also A. Luzio, "Frederico Gonzaga ostaggio alla corte di Giulio II," *Archivio della reale società romana di storia patria*, 9, 1886, 509ff., and esp. 578ff.; A. Rodocanachi, *Le Pontificat de Jules II 1503–1513*, Paris, 1928; A. Ademollo, *Alessandro VI, Giulio II, Leone X nel carnevale di Roma*, Florence, 1886, which reprints a poem of 1513 by J. J. Penni describing each float in detail; Jean Guiraud, *L'Etat pontifical après le grand schisme*, Bibliothèque des écoles françaises à Rome, 73, 1896; John A. F. Thomson, *Popes and Princes*, London, 1980, passim; and O'Malley, *Egidio of Viterbo*, 124ff.

24

Here I must demur at Panofsky's suggestion (*Studies*, 194ff.) that these four bound nude prisoners represent "the state of nature." He accordingly has the zone below the captives represent the four parts of the world, below the state of grace represented by the holy water in the basin on top. I would say that the four prisoners themselves represent the four corners of the world, as they existed in the bondage of paganism (there are garlands and sacrificial bucrania above them).

25

O'Malley, "Discourse," 286.

26

See Michael Mezzatesta, "The Facade of Leone Leoni's House in Milan," *Journal of the Society of Architectural Historians*, *44*, 1985, 233ff.

27

The finished tomb, erected in San Pietro in Vincoli in 1542–45 in drastically simplified form, seems still to echo Egidio's ideas. The niches are reduced to two in number and the *Captives* are eliminated. But the figures of Rachel and Leah, who fill those niches, continue to suggest the idea of restored property. In his sermon Egidio says that the restored province of Bologna is the antetype of Rachel (whose possessions, along with those of her sister Leah, were taken from her and then restored by God, Genesis 29.16, 29.30–36); see O'Malley, "Discourse," 338.

28

The cheeks turning into leaflike mustaches adapt a common antique device, copied earlier by Pinturicchio in the vaults of the Libreria Piccolomini, Siena Cathedral.

29

Charles de Tolnay and Paola Squellati Brizio, *Michelangelo e i Medici*, Casa Buonarroti, Florence, 1980, no. 25.

30

Or in Vitruvius's Greek, τροχίλος (5.3.2).

31

Elisabeth B. MacDougall, "Michelangelo and the Porta Pia," *Journal of the Society of Architectural Historians*, *19*, 1960, 97ff.; James S. Ackerman, *The Architecture of Michelangelo*, *1*, London, 1961, 114ff.; *2*, 125ff.

32

Touring Club Italiano, *Roma e dintorni*, Milan, 1976, 315. Cf. Armando Schiavo, *La Vita e le opere architettoniche di Michelangelo*, Rome, 1953, 265. MacDougall denies the possibility of this parodistic intent on the grounds that Michelangelo sketched somewhat similar details for the Ricetto of the Medici Library and also for the Library itself (MacDougall, "Porta Pia," figure 16). But these are all Medici commissions. The Florentine Medici were as much fair game as the Milanese. Punning on the Medici as *medici* was an emblematic commonplace. Cf. Janet Cox Rearick, *Dynasty and Destiny in Medici Art,* Princeton, 1984, 39, 150ff., 248.

33

Schiavo, *Vita,* 265.

34

Fra Giocondo's drawing of a caryatid head bearing an entablature in Uffizi UA 2050v may also be based on Vitruvius.

35

Commissioned from Fabio Calvo. But Calvo is way behind Fra Giocondo in scholarship, and he manhandles the Greek names for moldings and ornaments. Cf. Vincenzo Fontana and Paolo Morachiello, eds., *Vitruvio e Raffaello. Il "De Architectura" di Vitruvio nella traduzione inedita di Fabio Calvo Ravennate,* Rome, 1975, 16ff., 25ff. Raphael annotated in his own hand the version of the manuscript that is now in the Bayerische Staatsbibliothek, Munich; Fontana and Morachiello, 26n., and C. R. Frommel, Stefano Ray, and Manfredo Tafuri, *Raffaello architetto,* Rome, 1984, 379ff., and 3.3.1.

36

Fontana and Morachiello, 26ff.

37

It was also at this time, the mid-teens, when he was painting the Stanza d'Eliodoro, that Raphael made his most important use of "caryatids." These painted figures support the main scenes on the dado all around the room. For studies for these, see Oxford, Ashmolean P II 569B, and Louvre, Raphael inv. n. 3877. However, these "caryatids" are all non-Vitruvian *Stützfiguren.*

38

Pasquale Rotondi, *Il Palazzo ducale di Urbino, 1,* Urbino, 1950, 263ff; 291ff.

39

John Pope-Hennessy, *Raphael,* New York, 1970, 85ff.

40

The Sistine ceiling dates from 1508–12, the *Disputà* from 1511–12, and the *Moses* itself from 1515–16.

41

H. Pfeiffer, "Zur Ikonographie des Raphaels *Disputà.* Egidio da Viterbo und die christlich-platonische Konzeption der Stanza della Segnatura," *Miscellanea historiae pontificiae, 37,* Rome, 1975.

42

For more on Vitruvius's influence on the *School of Athens,* see Richard Brilliant, "Intellectual Giants: A Classical Topos and *The School of Athens," Source: Notes in the History of Art, 3, 4,* 1984, 1ff. Not long afterward another artist, Marcantonio Raimondi, paid his homage to the caryatid and Persian porticoes in a drawing of the 1520s. Cf. Frommel, Ray, and Tafuri, *Raffaello architetto*, no. 3.4.5. Here the two structures are combined: there is a lower Doric order of twenty-foot-high Persian satraps, with an upper story at similar scale of Ionic caryatids—once again *Stützfiguren* rather than the prisoners Vitruvius describes, probably reflecting Fra Giocondo's woodcuts. Pausanias's description of the Persian portico says that Artemisia, Queen of Helicarnassus, who showed particular ferocity as an ally of Xerxes against Greece, was portrayed in the Persian portico (3.11.3); no doubt the large female head in Marcantonio's drawing repesents her. (However, Pausanias adds that Mardonius, one of the chief Persian generals, was also portrayed.)

43

Frommel, "Capella Iulia," 50.

6

Cesariano, The *Vitruvius Teutsch*, and Sambin

1

Vitruvius: De architectura libri decem, ed. Cesare Cesariano, Como, 1521, lxi.

2

But much of the humanity of the Greek βάσις, the stepping, dancing, and standing of the human being, is left out in *gradum*.

3

Cesariano, 1.1.5.

4

For kneeling caryatids in antiquity see, Evamaria Schmidt, *Geschichte der Karyatide*, Würzburg, 1982, 121.

5

One good Vitruvius manuscript, Harleian 2767 (eighth century), British Library, London, seems to agree. It gives *Caria* instead of *Caryae* in 1.1.5. I thank J. J. Pollitt for pointing this out to me.

6

Or else he was thinking of Romanesque capitals, possibly to be found within the building in Cesariano's time, that actually were carved as heads. But if they ever existed, no such capitals are visible today, nor are they recorded in A. Calderini, G. Chierici, et al., *La Basilica di San Lorenzo Maggiore in Milano*, Milan, 1951.

7

This, and allied conceptions in Serlio and Lomazzo, are explored in my *Pythagorean Palaces: Magic and Architecture in the Italian Renaissance*, Ithaca, 1976, 109ff. and passim.

8

See Schmidt, *Karyatide,* 11ff.

9

Robert Garland, *The Greek Way of Death,* Ithaca, 1985, 55. Walter Burkert, *Homo necans: The Anthropology of Ancient Greek Sacrificial Ritual and Myth,* Berkeley, 1983, 165. For herms in the Renaissance, see Eugene J. Johnson, "Studies on the Use of Herms in 16th-Century Architecture in Italy," MA thesis, New York University, Institute of Fine Arts, 1963.

10

Edgar Wind, "Aenigma termini," *Journal of the Warburg and Courtauld Institutes, 1,* 1937–38, 66ff.

11

Pollux Grammaticus, ed. Bethe, Leipzig, 1900, 2.132.

12

On the other hand, the word could also be associated with ἄτλας, not enduring or daring, and ἀτλησία, incompetent.

13

Erik Forssmann, *Dorisch, jonisch, korinthisch: Studien über den Gebrauch der Säulenordnungen in der Architektur des 16.–18 hunderts,* Uppsala, 1961, and *Säule und Ornament,* Uppsala, 1956; Georg Weise, "Vitalismo, animismo e panpsichismo nella decorazione del cinquecento e del seicento," *Critica d'arte, 6,* 1959, 375ff., and *7,* 1960, 85ff.

14

Ambroise Paré, *Des monstres et prodiges* [1573], ed. Jean Céard, Geneva, 1971.

15

Jean Céard, *La Nature et les prodiges,* Geneva, 1977, 437ff.

16

Céard, *Prodiges,* 229ff.

17

See also Henri David, *De Sluter à Sambin, 2,* Paris, 1932, 401ff.

18

Vincenzo Cartari, *Imagini delli dei de gl'antichi,* Venice, 1647, 94.

19

Cartari, *Imagini,* 184.

20

Cartari, *Imagini,* 231.

21

Richard Broxton Onians, *The Origins of European Thought about the Body, . . . ,* Cambridge, 1951, 122.

22

Cartari, *Imagini*, 287.

23

Giovanni Paolo Lomazzo, *Trattato dell'arte de la pittura* [1584], Hildesheim, 1968, 421. Lomazzo's descriptions of Termini (413ff.) sound as if he had in mind the illustrations in the *Vitruvius Teutsch* and Sambin.

24

Sambin was a prolific designer of buildings and furniture. His part of France, around Dijon, is still full of sixteenth- and seventeenth-century buildings that reflect his brand of stylography. The Maison des Caryatides of 1603 in Dijon has a piano nobile and upper floor decorated with figures resembling Cesariano's Persian captives. In an upper room, with a gable, caryatids make a small domestic temple. The Maison Milsand, in the same city, is a veritable city of caryatids.

Conclusion

1

Barbaro does note that the Persian portico is related to the practice of raising trophies; he adds, however, that it was erected not literally out of captured weapons but with money received from their sale. Daniele Barbaro, ed., *De architectura libri decem*, Venice, 1556, 11. Another Vitruvian in Barbaro's category is Bernardino Baldi, whose 1612 *De verborum vitruvianorum significatione* also concentrates on philology.

2

Visionary Architects. Boullée, Ledoux, Lequeu, Houston, 1968 [exhibition catalogue], no. 121. BN Estampes Ha80a.

3

Mount Vernon: A Handbook, Mount Vernon, 1985, 37. The window dates from 1773ff.

4

For instance Allan Greenberg's Mount Vernon-based house in Connecticut. Paul Goldberger, "In Perpetuum," *Architectural Record*, 174, mid-April, 1986, 172ff.

Bibliography

Ackerman, James S. *The Architecture of Michelangelo*. London, 1961.

Ademollo, A. *Alessandro, Giulio e il carnevale*. Rome, 1967.

Anderson, J. K. *Hunting in the Ancient World*. Berkeley, 1985.

Ashmole, Bernard. *Architect and Sculptor in Classical Greece*. London, 1972.

Baldi, Bernardino. *De verborum vitruvianorum significatione*. Urbino, 1612. See also Daniele Barbaro.

Bammer, A. *Die Architektur des jüngeren Artemision von Ephesos*. Wiesbaden, 1972.

Barbaro, Daniele, ed. *Vitruvius*. Venice, 1556; Urbino, 1557. Some copies include Baldi's *De verborum vitruvianorum*.

Baumann, Hellmut. *Die griechiesche Pflanzenwelt in Mythos, Kunst, und Literatur*. Munich, 1982.

Bennett, Florence Mary. *Religious Cults Associated with Amazons*. New York, 1967.

Berve, H., H. Gruben, and M. Hirmer. *Greek Temples, Theaters and Shrines*. New York, n.d.

Betts, Richard J. "On the Chronology of Francesco di Giorgio's Treatises: New Evidence from an Unpublished Manuscript." *Journal of the Society of Architectural Historians*, *36*, 1977, 3ff.

Bickermann, E. "Alexandre le Grand et les villes d'Asie." *Revue des études grecques*, *47*, 1934, 346ff.

Birnbaum, A. "Vitruvius und die griechische Architektur." *Denkschrift des akademie der Wissenschaften*. Vienna, 1914.

Blinkenberg, Christian. *Le Temple de Paphos* [*Det Kgl. Danske Videnskabernes Selskab.*] *Historisk-filologiske Meddelelser*, 9.2. Copenhagen, 1924.

Boëthius, Axel. "Vitruvius and the Roman Architecture of his Age." Δράγμα *M. P. Nilsson dedicatum*. Acta institutae Romanae Regni Sueciae, 2, 1, Lund, 1939, 114ff.

Boetticher, Carl. *Der Baumkultus der Hellenen*. Berlin, 1856.

Brilliant, Richard. "Intellectual Giants: A Classical Topos and *The School of Athens*." *Source: Notes in the History of Art*, *3*, 4, 1984, 1ff.

Burkert, Walter. "Glaube und Verhalten: Zeichengehalt und Wirkungsmacht von Opferritualen." *Entretiens sur l'antiquité classique, 27. Le Sacrifice dans l'antiquité.* Fondation Hardt, Geneva, 1980, 91ff.

———. *Greek Religion.* Cambridge, Mass., 1985.

———. *Homo necans: The Anthropology of Ancient Greek Sacrificial Ritual and Myth* [1972]. Berkeley, 1983.

Calame, Claude. *Les Choeurs des jeunes filles en Grèce archaique.* Rome, 1977.

Calderini, A., G. Chierici, et al. *La Basilica di San Lorenzo Maggiore in Milano.* Milan, 1951.

Callebat, L., P. Bouet, Ph. Fleury, M. Zuinghedau. *Vitruve. De Architectura. Concordance.* Hildesheim, 1984.

Carlier-Détienne, Jeannie, "Les Amazones font la guerre et l'amour." *L'Ethnographie,* 1980–81, 11ff.

Cartari, Vincenzo. *Imagini delli dei de gl'antichi.* Venice, 1647; repr. ed. W. Koschatzky, Graz, 1967.

Casabona, Jean. *Recherches sur le vocabulaire des sacrifices en grec, des origines à la fin de l'époque classique.* Aix-en-Provence, 1966.

Cassola, Filippo. *La Ionia nel mondo micenea.* Naples, 1957.

———. "I Cari nella tradizione greca." *La Parola del passato, 12,* fasc. 54, 1957, 192ff.

Céard, Jean. *La Nature et les prodiges.* Geneva, 1977.

Cesariano, Cesare. *Vitruvius: De architectura libri decem.* Como, 1521.

Charles-Picard, Gilbert. *Les Trophées romains.* Paris, 1957.

Chipiez, Charles. *Histoire critique des ordres grecs.* Paris, 1876.

Ciapponi, Lucia A. "Il 'De Architectura' di Vitruvio nel primo umanesimo." *Italia medioevale e umanistica, 3,* 1960, 59ff.

———. "Fra Giocondo da Verona and his Edition of Vitruvius." *Journal of the Warburg and Courtauld Institutes, 47,* 1984, 72ff.

Claus, Adolph. "De Dianae antiquissima apud Graecos natura." Diss., Breslau, 1881.

Condivi, Ascanio. "Vita di Michelangelo." In Paolo d'Ancona, et al., *Michelangelo.* Milan, 1964.

David, Henri. *De Sluter à Sambin.* Paris, 1932.

Delivorrias, A. *Attische Giebelskulpturen und Akrotere des fünften Jahrhunderts (Tübingen Studien zur Archäologie und Kunstgeschichte, 1).* Tübingen, 1974.

Demangel, R. *La Frise ionique.* Paris, 1933.

Detienne, Marcel, and Jean-Pierre Vernant. *La Cuisine du sacrifice en pays grec.* Paris, 1979.

de Tolnay, Charles. *The Tomb of Julius II.* Princeton, 1954.

de Tolnay, Charles, and Paola Squellati Brizio. *Michelangelo e i Medici.* Casa Buonarroti, Florence, 1980.

De Waele, J. "Der Entwurf der dorischen Tempel von Paestum." *Archäologische Anzeiger,* 1980, 267ff.

Dinsmoor, W. B. *The Architecture of Ancient Greece.* London and New York, 1950.

———. "The Greek Temples at Paestum." *Memoirs of the American Academy at Rome, 20,* 1950.

Donaldson, T. L. *Architectura numismatica.* London, 1859.

Douglas, Mary. *Purity and Danger.* London, 1966.

Ducrey, Pierre. *Le Traitement des prisonniers de guerre dans la Grèce antique.* Paris, 1968.

Ebhardt, Bodo. *Die zehn Bücher der Architektur des Vitruv und ihre Herausgeber (seit 1484)* [1918]. Ossining, NY, 1962.

Eitrem, S. *Beiträge zur griechischen Religionsgeschichte. 1. Der vor-dorische Widdergott.* Christiania, 1910.

Engel, Wilhelm H. *Kypros, eine Monographie.* Berlin, 1841.

Evans, A. L. "Mycenaean Tree and Pillar Cult and its Mediterranean Relations." *Journal of Hellenic Studies, 21,* 1901, 99ff.

Fairbanks, A. *Athenian Lekythoi.* New York, 1914.

Ferguson, John. *Religions of the Roman Empire.* Ithaca, 1970.

Ferri, Silvio. *Vitruvio, Architettura dai libri i–vii.* Rome, 1960.

Fontana, Vincenzo, and Paolo Morachiello, eds. *Vitruvio e Raffaello. Il "De Architectura" di Vitruvio nella traduzione inedita di Fabio Calvo Ravennate.* Rome, 1975.

Forssmann, Erik. *Dorisch, jonisch, korinthisch. Studien über den Gebrauch der Säulenordnungen in der Architektur des 16.–18 hunderts.* Uppsala, 1961.

———. *Saüle und Ornament.* Uppsala, 1956.

Frazer, James G. *The Golden Bough: Taboo and the Perils of the Soul.* 3rd ed. London, 1911.

Freud, Sigmund. *Totem and Taboo* [1913]. New York, 1950.

Frey, K., ed. *Die Handzeichnungen Michelagniolos Buonarroti.* Berlin, 1897.

Frommel, Christoph Luitpold. "'Cappella Iulia:' Die Grabkapelle Papst Julius II in Neu-St. Peter." *Zeitschrift für Kunstgeschichte, 40,* 1977, 26ff.

———. "Die Peterskirche unter Papst Julius II im Lichte neuer Dokumente." *Römisches Jahrbuch für Kunstgeschichte, 16,* 1976, 57ff.

Frommel, Christoph Luitpold, Stefano Ray, and Manfredo Tafuri. *Raffaello architetto.* Rome, 1984.

Gardner, E. A., D. G. Hogarth, M. R. James, and R. E. Smith. "Excavations on Cyprus, 1887–1888." *Journal of the Hellenic Society, 9,* 1888, 270ff.

Garland, Robert. *The Greek Way of Death.* Ithaca, 1985.

Garzoni, Bartolommeo. *Il Serraglio degli stupori del mondo.* Venice, 1613.

Gernet, Louis. *Anthropologie de la Grèce antique.* Paris, 1968.

Gori, A. F. [and G. B. Passeri]. *Thesaurus gemmarum antiquarum astriferarum.* . . . Florence, 1750.

Gros, Pierre. "Vitruve: l'architecture et sa théorie des études récentes." *Aufstieg und Niedergang der römischen Welt, 2,* 30, 1, 1982, 659ff.

Gruben, Gottfried. *Die Tempel der Griechen.* Munich, 1986.

Guglia, E. "Die Türkenfrage auf dem Laterankonzil." *Mitteilungen des Instituts für Osterreichische Geschichtsforschung, 21,* 1900, 684ff.

Guicciardini, Francesco. *La Historia di Italia.* Florence, 1561.

Guiraud, Jean. *L'Etat pontifical après le grand schisme.* Bibliothèque des écoles françaises à Rome, *73,* 1896.

Gullini, G. "Soll'origine del fregio dorico." *Memorie dell'accademia delle scienze di Torino.* Classe di scienze morali, storiche e filologiche, ser. 4a, no. 31, Turin, 1974.

Helbig, Walter. *Führer durch die öffentlicher Sammlungen klassischer Altertümer in Rom, 2.* Tübingen, 1966.

Herrmann, Klaus. "Zum Dekor dorischer Kapitelle." *Architectura, 13,* 1, 1983, 1ff.

Hersey, George. *Pythagorean Palaces: Magic and Architecture in the Italian Renaissance.* Ithaca, 1976.

———. "The Classical Orders of Architecture as Totems in Vitruvian Myth." *Umanesimo a Roma nel quattrocento.* Rome/New York, 1984, 213ff.

Hexter, H. "Hetairai." *Reallexikon für Antike und Christentum, 3,* 1957, 1154ff.

———. "Des Soziologie der antike Prostitution im Lichte des heidnischen und christliche Schrifttums." *Jahrbuch für Antike und Christentums, 3,* 1960, 70ff.

Hibbard, Howard. *Michelangelo.* New York, 1974.

Hill, G. F. *A Catalogue of the Greek Coins of Cyprus.* London, 1904.

———. *A History of Cyprus.* Cambridge, 1940–52.

Hock, G. "Griechische Weihegebräuche." Diss., Munich, 1905.

Hoepfner, W. "Zum ionischen Kapitell bei Hermogenes und Vitruv." *Mitteilungen des deutschen archäologischen Instituts, Athen, 83,* 1968, 213ff.

Hubert, H., and M. Mauss. *Sacrifice, Its Nature and Function* [1899]. Chicago, 1964.

James, E. O. *Sacrifice and Sacrament.* London, 1962.

Janson, A. J. *Het Antike Tropaion*. Ghent, 1957.

Jatta, C. *Le Rappresentazioni figurate delle provincie romane*. Rome, 1908.

Jeppesen, Kristian. "Where was the so-called Erechtheion?" *American Journal of Archaeology*, *83*, 1979, 381ff.

Johnson, Eugene J. "Studies on the Use of Herms in Sixteenth-Century Architecture." MA Thesis, Institute of Fine Arts, New York University, 1963.

Kähler, H. *Das griechischen Metopenbild*. Munich, 1949.

Karageorghis, Vassos, and Jean des Gagniers. *La Céramique Chypriote de style figuré. Age du Fer (1050–500 av.J.-C.)*. Rome, 1974.

————. *The Civilisation of Prehistoric Cyprus*. Athens, c. 1976.

Kirk, G. S. "Some Methodological Pitfalls in the Study of Ancient Greek Sacrifice." *Entretiens sur l'antiquité classique*, *27*. *Le Sacrifice dans l'antiquité*. Fondation Hardt, Geneva, 1980.

Klinz, A. 'ΙΕΡΟΣ ΓΑΜΟΣ. Halle, 1933.

Klusemann, K. *Das Bauopfer*. Graz-Hamburg, 1919.

Lapalus, E. *Le Fronton sculpté en Grèce, des origines à la fin du IVme siècle*. Paris, 1947.

Lawrence, A. W. *Greek Architecture*. 4th ed. Harmondsworth, 1983.

Lenz, C. G. *Die Göttin von Paphos auf alten Bildwerken und Baphomet*. Gotha, 1808.

Lévi-Strauss, Claude. *Totemism*. Boston, 1962.

Lomazzo, Giovanni Paolo. *Trattato dell'arte de la pittura* [1584]. Hildesheim, 1968.

Loulloupis, M. C. "Mycenaean Horns of Consecration in Cyprus." *Acts of the International Archaeological Symposium "The Relations between Cyprus and Crete, ca. 2000–500 BC."* Nicosia, 1979, 102ff.

Lowic, Lawrence. "The Meaning and Significance of the Human Analogy in Francesco di Giorgio's Trattato." *Journal of the Society of Architectural Historians*, *62*, 1983, 25ff.

Luynes, H. de. *Numismatique et inscriptions cypriotes*. Paris, 1852.

Luzio, A. "Federico Gonzaga ostaggio alla corte di Giulio II." *Archivio della reale deputazione romana di storia patria*. 1886, 580ff.

MacDougall, Elisabeth B. "Michelangelo's Porta Pia." *Journal of the Society of Architectural Historians*, *19*, 1960, 97ff.

Maier, F. G. "Temple of Aphrodite at Kouklia (Old Paphos)." *RDAC*, 1965–67, 86ff.

————. "The Temple of Aphrodite at Old Paphos." *RDAC*, 1975, 67ff.

————. *Brief History and Description of Old Paphos (Kuklia)*. Nicosia, n.d.

————. "The Paphian Shrine of Aphrodite and Crete." *International Archaeological Symposium "The Relations between Cyprus and Crete, ca. 2000–500 BC."* Nicosia, 1978, 228ff.

Martini, Francesco di Giorgio. *Trattati di architettura, ingegneria e arte militare, 1.* Ed. Corrado Maltese. Milan, 1967.

Mazzocchi, Alessio. *Commentariorum in regii Herculanensis musei aeneas tabulas heracleenses.* Naples, 1754.

Merkelbach, R. "Gefesselte Götter," *Antaios, 13,* 1971, 549ff.

Mezzatesta, Michael. "The Facade of Leone Leoni's House in Milan," *Journal of the Society of Architectural Historians, 44,* 1985, 233ff.

Moulinier, Louis. *Le Pur et l'impur dans la pensée des grecs, d'Homère à Aristote. Etudes et commentaires, 11.* Paris, 1952.

Münter, D. Friedrich. *Der Tempel der himmlischen Göttin zu Paphos.* Copenhagen, 1824.

Myres, J. L. *Handbook of the Cesnola Collection of Antiquities from Cyprus.* New York, 1914.

Nilsson, Martin P. *Geschichte der griechische Religion.* Munich, 1955–61.

Noack, Ferdinand. "Triumph und Triumphbogen." *Vorträge der Bibliothek Warburg, 5,* 1925–26, 147ff.

Ohnefalsch-Richter, Max. *Kypros, die Bibel und Homer.* Berlin, 1893.

Onians, Richard Broxton. *The Origins of European Thought about the Body, the Mind, the Soul, the World, Time, and Fate. . . .* Cambridge, 1951.

O'Malley, John, ed. "Fulfillment of the Christian Golden Age under Pope Julius II: Text of a Discourse by Giles of Viterbo." *Traditio, 25,* 1969, 265ff.

————. *Giles of Viterbo on Church and Reform.* Leiden, 1968.

O'Reilly, Clare. "'Maximus Caesar et Pontifex Maximus': Giles of Viterbo Proclaims the Alliance between Emperor Maximilian I and Pope Julius II." *Augustiniana, 22,* 1972, 80ff.

Ornament and Architecture: Renaissance Drawings, Prints and Books. Brown University, Providence, Rhode Island, 1980.

Panofsky, Erwin. "The First Two Projects of Michelangelo's Tomb of Julius II." *Art Bulletin, 19,* 1937, 561ff.

————. *Studies in Iconology* [1939]. New York, 1972.

Paschini, Pio. *Roma nel Rinascimento.* Bologna, 1940.

Pastor, Ludwig. *The History of the Popes, 6.* London, 1898.

Paton, J. M., and G. P. Stevens. *The Erechtheum.* Cambridge, Mass., 1927.

Pfeiffer, H. "Zur Ikonographie des Raphaels *Disputà*. Egidio da Viterbo und die christlich-platonische Konzeption der Stanza della Segnatura." *Miscellanea historiae pontificiae* [Rome], *37*, 1975.

Philandrier, Guillaume, ed. *Vitruvius.* 1550.

Picard, G. C. *Les trophées romains.* Paris, 1957.

Piccaluga, Giulia. "L'Olocausto di Patrai." *Entretiens sur l'antiquité classique, 27. Le sacrifice dans L'antiquité.* Fondation Hardt, Geneva, 1980, 243ff.

Plommer, Hugh. "Vitruvian Studies." *Annals of the British School at Athens* [London], *65*, 1970, 182ff.

Pollitt, J. J. *The Ancient View of Greek Art.* New Haven, 1974; Munich, 1982.

Pontrandolfo, Angela. "Paestum and its Archaeological History," in *Paestum and the Doric Revival, 1750–1830.* National Academy of Design, New York, 1986, 51ff.

Pope-Hennessy, John. *Raphael.* New York, 1970.

————. *Italian High Renaissance and Baroque Sculpture.* London, 1963.

Pritchett, W. K. *The Greek State at War.* Two vols. Berkeley, 1979.

Rhomaios, K. Καρυατίδες, ΠΕΛΟΠΟΝΝΕΣΙΑΚΑ, 3–4, 1958/59, 376ff.

Ribichini, Sergio. *Adonis.* Rome, 1980.

Robertson, D. S. *A Handbook of Greek and Roman Architecture.* Cambridge, 1929. 2nd ed., Cambridge, 1943.

Rodocanachi, A. *Le Pontificat de Jules II, 1503–13.* Paris, 1928.

Rousseau, Jean-Jacques. *Essai sur l'origine des langues.* Paris, 1783.

Rykwert, Joseph. "On an (Egyptian?) Misreading of Francesco di Giorgio's." *Res 1*, Spring 1981, 78ff.

————. *On Adam's House in Paradise. The Idea of the Primitive Hut in Architectural History.* New York, c. 1972.

————. "The Corinthian Order." In Rykwert, *The Necessity of Artifice.* Cambridge, 1980, 33ff.

Sabbatucci, Dario. "Sacer." *Studi e materiali di storia delle religioni, 24–25*, 1952, 92ff.

Sambin, Hugues. *De la diversité des termes.* Lyon, 1572.

Scaglia, Giustina. *Il "Vitruvio Magliabecchiano" di Franceso di Giorgio Martini* (Documenti inediti di Cultura Toscana, 6), Florence, 1985.

Schaller-Harl, Friedrike. *Stützfiguren in der griechischen Kunst.* Vienna, 1973.

Schiavo, Armando. *La Vita e le opere architettoniche di Michelangelo.* Rome, 1953.

Schmidt, Evamaria. *Geschichte der Karyatide.* Würzburg, 1982.

Schmidt-Colinet, A. *Antike Stützfiguren.* Cologne, 1977.

Schnapp, A. "Pratiche ed immagini di caccia nella Grecia antica." *Dialoghi di archaeologia*, n.s. *1*, 1979, 36ff.

Schott, Auguste. "Akanthus." *Jahreshefte des Österreichischen Archäologischen Instituts, 44*, 1959, 54ff.

Schultz, Bernard. *Art and Anatomy in Renaissance Italy.* Ann Arbor, 1985.

Schwenn, Friedrich. "Die Menschenopfer bei den Griechen und Römern." *Religionsgeschichtliche Versuche und Vorarbeiten, 15*, 1915.

————. "Der Krieg in der griechischen Religion," *Archiv für Religionswissenschaft, 21,* 1922.

Schwoebel, Robert H. "Coexistence, Conversion, and the Crusade against the Turks." *Studies in the Renaissance, 12,* 1965, 164ff.

Scully, Vincent. *The Earth, The Temple, and the Gods.* New Haven, 1962; rev. ed., 1979.

Serlio, Sebastiano. *Livre extraordinaire de architecture de Sebastien Serlio. . . .* Lyon, 1551.

Simon, Erika. *Festivals of Attica.* Madison, Wis., 1983.

————. *Opfernde Götter.* Berlin, 1953.

Stengel, Paul. *Die griechischen Kultusaltertümer.* Munich, 1898.

Stuart-Jones, H. *A Catalogue of the Ancient Sculptures Preserved in the Municipal Collections of Rome. The Sculptures of the Palazzo dei Conservatori.* Oxford, 1926.

Summers, David. "Michelangelo on Architecture." *Art Bulletin, 54,* 1972, 146ff.

————. *Michelangelo and the Language of Art.* Princeton, 1981.

Toeppfer, J. *Attische Genealogie.* Berlin, 1889.

Tomlinson, R. A. "The Doric Order: Hellenistic Critics and Criticism." *Journal of Hellenic Studies, 83,* 1963, 133ff.

Vasari, Giorgio. *Vita di Michelangelo.* ed. Paola Barocchi. Milan/Naples, 1962.

Vernant, Jean-Pierre. "Théorie générale du sacrifice et mise à mort dans la θυσία grèque." *Entretiens sur l'antiquité classique, 27. Le Sacrifice dans l'antiquité.* Fondation Hardt, Geneva, 1980.

————. *Mythe et pensée chez les Grecs.* Paris, 1965.

Vico, Giambattista. *La Scienza nuova seconda.* Naples, 1744.

Visconti, Ennius Quirinus. *Musée Pie-Clémentin.* Milan, 1818.

Vitruvius Teutsch, 1549.

Vitruvius Pollio. *Il "De Architectura" di Vitruvio nella traduzione inedita di Fabio Calvo Ravennate,* ed. Vincenzo Fontana and Paolo Marachiello. Rome, 1975.

von Einem, Herbert. *Michelangelo, Bildhauer, Maler, Baumeister.* Berlin, 1973.

Weickert, C. *Das lesbische Kymation.* Leipzig, 1913.

Wesenberg, Burkhardt. "Die Kopien der Erechtheion Koren und die Frauen von Karyai." *Jahrbuch des Deutschen Archäologischen Instituts, 99,* 1984, 172ff.

Wiebenson, Dora, ed. *Architectural Theory and Practice from Alberti to Ledoux.* [Chicago], 1982.

Wiese, Georg. "Vitalismo, animismo e panpsichismo nella decorazione del cinquecento e del seicento." *Critica d'arte, 6,* 1959, 375ff. and 7, 1960, 85ff.

Westholm, Alfred. "The Paphian Temple of Aphrodite and Its Relation to Oriental Architecture." *Acta archaeologica* [Copenhagen], *4,* 1933, 217ff.

Wide, Sam. *Lakonische Kulte.* Leipzig, 1893.

Williger, Eduard. "Hagios. Untersuchungen zur Terminologie des Heiligen in den Hellenisch-Hellenistischen Religionen." *Religionsgeschichtliche Versuche und Vorarbeiten, 19,* 1922.

Woelcke, K. "Beiträge zur Geschichte der Tropaions." *Bonner Jahrbücher, 120,* 1911, 127ff.

Index